Progress-Monitoring Comprehension Strategy Assessments for Grades 3–4

Newmark Learning

629 Fifth Avenue • Pelham, NY • 10803

ISBN 978-1-60719-049-3

For ordering information, call Toll-Free 1-877-279-8388 or visit our Web site at www.newmarklearning.com.

Table of Contents

Grade 3	Grade 4

Introduction

Progress-Monitoring Comprehension Strategy Assessments for Grades 3-4 are a series of one-page assessments that you can administer periodically during the school year to monitor your students' growth as a result of comprehension strategy instruction or intervention. Each assessment includes a reading passage and two test items designed to measure one specific strategy. The assessments cover fifteen comprehension strategies (see the Table of Contents) with three assessments per strategy. The three assessments per strategy cover a range of reading levels for Grades 3–4. Administer the level of assessment that best meets your students' needs (the grade level of each assessment is indicated in parentheses next to the assessment title in the Table of Contents).

Assessment Level	Administer to the Following Students
Grade Three	Students in Grade 3 reading at levels 30–38 (N–O) Students in Grade 4 reading at levels 30–38 (N–O)
Grade Four	Students in Grade 4 reading at level 40 (Q–R) Students in Grade 5 reading at level 40 (Q–R)

You may wish to administer assessments after completing instruction in a particular strategy, or you may administer the assessments at other appropriate times, such as the end of each grading period. These pages may be used as reading assessments or listening assessments.

 ©2009 Newmark Learning, LLC

Administering and Scoring the Reading Comprehension Assessments

The Grade 3 and Grade 4 assessments are designed to be reading comprehension assessments. Each assessment consists of a one-page reading passage and a set of five questions. Three of the items are multiple-choice questions; the other two are short-answer questions that require students to write their own answers (most of these responses will be one to three sentences long).

Plan for about 15–20 minutes to administer an Ongoing Comprehension Strategy Assessment, but allow more time if needed.

To Administer an Ongoing Assessment

1. Make a copy of the assessment for each student.
2. Have students write their names and the date at the top of each test page.
3. Direct students to read each passage and answer the questions that go with it.
4. For each multiple-choice question, instruct students to choose the best answer and fill in the bubble beside the answer they choose.
5. For short-answer questions, have students write their responses (in phrases or complete sentences) on the lines provided.

Listening Comprehension

The Grades 3 and 4 Ongoing Assessments are intended primarily for use as written assessments of reading comprehension. However, they may also be used as measures of listening comprehension. To use these assessments for listening purposes, read the passage aloud to the student(s) and have the student(s) answer the questions. Students may respond by marking and writing their answers on the test page, or you may have students give oral responses. If you prefer, you may use two of the three Ongoing Assessments for each strategy for reading comprehension and the other for listening.

To Score the Ongoing Assessment

1. Refer to the appropriate Answer Key (see pages 98–102). The Answer Key provides the letter of the correct response for each multiple-choice question. The Answer Key also provides a sample correct response for each short-answer question.
2. Mark each question correct or incorrect on the test page. You may need to interpret the students' written responses and decide whether the responses are correct based on the sample answers in the Answer Key.
3. To find the total score, count the number of items answered correctly.

Using the Results

1. Use the results of the Ongoing Assessments to evaluate each student's understanding of the tested strategy or skill.

2. A student who understands and applies a given strategy should answer at least four of the five items correctly. A student who answers correctly fewer than four items may need additional instruction on a particular strategy.

3. Use the Scoring Chart to keep track of students' scores on the assessments during the school year. The record provides space for writing a student's score on each of the Strategy Assessments and for noting comments relevant to a student's progress in learning a particular strategy.

Directions: Read the passage. Then use the information from the passage to answer questions 1–5.

First on the Courts

Althea Gibson played many sports when she was young. Then someone taught her to play tennis. She knew it was the sport for her. She quit school to play tennis full time.

Gibson played in a black women's tennis league. She won many games. During this time, she also went back to school. She got her high school diploma.

In 1950, Gibson became the first African American woman to play in the U.S. Nationals. She lost the first set and won the second set. In the third set, she lost again. But she decided to keep trying.

Many tennis clubs did not let Gibson play because she was African American. Some hotels would not give her a room. But Gibson did not let this get her down. She kept playing hard. She wanted to be the best. Soon she started to win both singles and doubles matches. At the U.S. Nationals in 1956, though, she lost again.

The next year, Gibson's hard work paid off. She won the U.S. Nationals. She was named Female Athlete of the Year. She was the first African American to win that honor.

Althea Gibson's success made it easier for other African Americans, and other women, to succeed in sports. One great female tennis player was Billie Jean King. She said that many other women would have had a much harder time if not for Gibson. Althea Gibson showed them it could be done.

Name _____ Date_____

1. **Althea Gibson won the U.S. Nationals after many tries. What does that tell you about her character?**
   Ⓐ She did not like attention.   Ⓑ She was very shy.
   Ⓒ She was very smart.   Ⓓ She was very determined.

2. **Which detail shows that Althea Gibson faced hardship with bravery?**
   Ⓐ She kept playing even though clubs and hotels would not let her in.
   Ⓑ She went back to school and got her diploma.
   Ⓒ She played both singles and doubles matches.
   Ⓓ She was named Female Athlete of the Year.

3. **What do Billie Jean King's words tell you about Gibson?**
   Ⓐ She was scared but overcame her fear.
   Ⓑ She was very lucky to have done as well as she did.
   Ⓒ She eased the way for other women in sports.
   Ⓓ She was unhappy most of the time.

4. **How can you tell that Althea Gibson always wanted to improve herself? Give one detail from the passage to support this idea.**

   _____

   _____

5. **Do you think Althea Gibson is a sports legend? Use information about her character to support your answer.**

   _____

   _____

Directions: Read the passage. Then use the information from the passage to answer questions 1–5.

The Contest

Jessie paid for her lunch. She took her change and put it on her tray. Then she sat down to eat with her friends.

"Look at your quarter!" Jon said. "There's a horse on it! This is so cool!"

Jessie looked closely at the quarter. It was true! On one side there was a picture of George Washington, and on the other side was a horse. Above the horse was the word *Kentucky*.

After lunch, Jessie and Jon showed the quarter to Mr. Cho. "This is a state quarter," he told them. "The first state quarters were made in 1999. Soon there will be a special quarter for every state."

"Let's have a contest!" Jon said to Jessie. "Let's see who can find more state quarters, but each one has to be different."

That night, Jessie looked at the coins in her bank. She asked Dad to check the coins in his pockets. She even looked in the little coin cup in the car. All together she found seven different quarters. Jessie studied each one. They were so interesting! Each one showed something important about the state. Jessie got some paper and made a neat list of the seven states. Then she drew a picture of each quarter.

Jon told his family about the contest. "Let's all look for quarters!" he said. Jon's family all jumped up to look. Jon found three quarters, and his mother and father gave him ten more. His brother gave him five, and his sister gave him one. Jon counted all the quarters. "I have 19 quarters, and there are 13 different ones! I'll win the contest for sure," he said.

Name _____ Date_____

1. What detail from the passage tells you that Jessie enjoys learning things?

Ⓐ Jessie looked closely at the quarter. It was true!

Ⓑ Jessie studied each one. They were so interesting!

Ⓒ After lunch, Jessie and Jon showed the quarter to Mr. Cho.

Ⓓ That night, Jessie looked at the coins in her bank.

2. What did Jon like best about finding state quarters?

Ⓐ finding out about horses

Ⓑ getting his family involved in the fun

Ⓒ winning the contest

Ⓓ seeing how each quarter was different

3. Which word best describes Jon?

Ⓐ sly

Ⓑ friendly

Ⓒ curious

Ⓓ enthusiastic

4. How do you think Jessie will feel when she finds out Jon has more quarters?

_____

_____

5. Describe Jessie's character, using details from the passage.

_____

_____

Name _____ Date _____

Directions: Read the passage. Then use the information from the passage to answer questions 1–5.

Elizabeth Cady Stanton

Today, we take it for granted that women can vote. This was not always so. Women won the right to vote, thanks to leaders like Elizabeth Cady Stanton. She fought for equal rights for women. She wanted women to have the same rights as men.

Elizabeth Cady was born in 1815. Her father was a judge. Elizabeth studied law in his office. She also studied Greek, Latin, and math. She got the best education a woman could get at the time.

After graduating from school, Cady met the man who would be her husband. His name was Henry Stanton. He worked hard to end slavery in the United States. He and Elizabeth were married in 1840. Then they went to the World's Anti-Slavery Convention in London, England. There, Cady Stanton met Lucretia Mott. Mott was denied a seat in the meeting hall. In fact, none of the women got a seat. This convinced Cady Stanton that women should hold their own meeting for women's rights.

In 1848, Cady Stanton led the first women's rights convention. It took place in Seneca Falls, New York. Cady Stanton wrote statements for a Declaration of Rights. She presented them at this meeting.

Elizabeth Cady Stanton fought for women's rights for the rest of her life. She died in 1897 at the age of 82.

Name _____ Date _____

1. **For much of her life, Elizabeth Cady Stanton's main goal was to _____.**
   - Ⓐ vote for a president
   - Ⓑ gain equal rights for women
   - Ⓒ become a lawyer
   - Ⓓ hold a meeting for women only

2. **Based on the information in the passage, which words best describe the character of Elizabeth Cady Stanton?**
   - Ⓐ angry and fierce
   - Ⓑ generous and caring
   - Ⓒ humorous and sharp
   - Ⓓ intelligent and determined

3. **Which fact supports the character traits you chose in question two?**
   - Ⓐ She took for granted that women could vote.
   - Ⓑ Her father was a judge and she got a good education.
   - Ⓒ She studied law and fought for women's rights.
   - Ⓓ Her husband, Henry Stanton, fought to end slavery.

4. **What convinced Elizabeth Cady Stanton to hold a convention for women's rights?**

   _____

   _____

5. **Elizabeth Cady Stanton was considered a daring and dedicated leader. Give one or two details from the passage to support this statement.**

   _____

   _____

Directions: Read the passage. Then use the information from the passage to answer questions 1–5.

Buried Alive

Jen and Kurt got off the chairlift and skied to the top of the trail for their last run of the day. They were both exhausted.

Suddenly, they spotted a skier slipping past a fence put up by the Ski Patrol. A sign on the fence warned DANGER–KEEP OUT!

Within minutes, a wave of snow rushed down the mountain and covered the skier. There was no sign of him as the snow continued to rumble down the slope.

"Oh, no," cried Jen, "I think that skier's in serious trouble." She reached for her radio and called the Ski Patrol.

"Ski Patrol here," her father responded.

"Dad, it's Jen. Kurt and I are standing at the top of Meadow Trail. A skier just went down the fenced-off trail. He set off an avalanche, and he's buried!"

"I'll send the rescue team," said Dad.

The team arrived within minutes. The rescue dog located the spot where the skier was buried. With small metal shovels, the rescue workers dug out the skier as quickly as they could. He seemed to be okay as they strapped him into a sled and started down the mountain.

"Great work, kids," Dad said proudly.

Name _____ Date_____

1. Where does this story take place?

Ⓐ at a hospital   Ⓑ in a classroom

Ⓒ in a forest   Ⓓ on a mountain

2. What was the problem in this story?

Ⓐ Jen and Kurt were really tired.

Ⓑ They could not ski the last run of the day.

Ⓒ A skier got buried in an avalanche.

Ⓓ The rescue team could not find the skier

3. How did Jen feel when she saw the skier disappear?

Ⓐ excited   Ⓑ worried

Ⓒ angry   Ⓓ proud

4. How did the dog help the rescue team?

_____

_____

5. What happened to the skier at the end of the story?

_____

_____

Directions: *Read the passage. Then use the information from the passage to answer questions 1–5.*

A Long Week

Mama had been sick for six days. Rebecca made Papa's supper and went to sit by Mama. "You need to eat, too," Papa said. "Come and eat supper."

Rebecca was too worried to eat, and she was so tired! She just wanted to sit and watch Mama sleep. She hoped that Mama would soon wake up and smile. But Mama had not smiled for a long time. Mama had not smiled for six whole days.

For almost a week Rebecca had cared for Mama. She washed Mama's hot face. She brought cool water for Mama to drink. She sat by Mama's bed and read her stories. But Mama did not even hear. Mama just slept and slept.

While Mama slept, Rebecca made a fire every morning. She cooked breakfast and supper for Papa. She washed the plates and cups. She fed the pigs and chickens. She watered the garden. Each time she finished a job, she told Mama. But Mama did not seem to hear.

The next morning, Mama was no better. Her fever seemed worse than ever. Papa looked worried. "We need the doctor, but it is a long ride to town. I do not want to leave you and Mama for so long."

"I will get the doctor," Rebecca said. "I can ride my pony and be back before dark."

Name _____ Date_____

1. When does this story take place?

Ⓐ a long time ago

Ⓑ a few years ago

Ⓒ in the present

Ⓓ far in the future

2. What is the main problem in this story?

Ⓐ It is a long way to town.

Ⓑ Rebecca has too much work to do.

Ⓒ Mama is very sick.

Ⓓ Papa does not want to leave Rebecca and Mama.

3. Where does this story take place?

Ⓐ in a city

Ⓑ on a farm

Ⓒ in a town

Ⓓ on a boat

4. Why was Rebecca so concerned about Mama's illness? Give two details about Mama's illness that made Rebecca worry.

_____

_____

5. What will Papa and Rebecca most likely do next?

_____

_____

Directions: Read the passage. Then use the information from the passage to answer questions 1–5.

The Wall

Everyone on the field watched as Persa sprinted toward the ball. She was tiny, fierce, and fast. In her bright red jersey, she became a blur as she raced down the field and kicked the ball deep into the blue team's territory.

Gwen also ran down the field, trying to stay close to the ball. She pushed herself as hard as she could, but she still felt big and clumsy. Gwen was clearly the slowest runner on the red team. She had just reached the midfield line when Persa approached the blue team's goal. With a furious kick of the ball, Persa booted it toward the goal, but the blue team's goalie leaped into the air and made a beautiful save.

Then the goalie trotted out from the goal and passed the ball to one of her team members, Marisabel, who turned and charged up the field. Gwen started running back toward her goal.

As she neared the goalkeeper's box in front of her net, Gwen turned to face the action. Marisabel shot the ball toward the goal, but Gwen was ready. She crossed her arms and leaned back. The ball hit her with a thud and dropped to the ground, and a huge cheer rose from her team. Then a small red blur whizzed by. It was Persa smiling toward Gwen. "Good job!" she panted as she streaked by.

Gwen blocked many more shots that day, using her size and strength to advantage. By the end of the game, her teammates were shouting, "You can't get past The Wall!" Gwen grinned as she listened to the chanting of her teammates. She had found a place for herself on the team.

Name _____ Date _____

1. Where does this story take place?

Ⓐ on a baseball field

Ⓑ in a classroom

Ⓒ on a soccer field

Ⓓ in a gym

2. What is the theme of this story?

Ⓐ Different people have different valuable skills to offer.

Ⓑ Children should be taught to work together rather than compete with one another.

Ⓒ A good sense of humor can help you overcome your problems.

Ⓓ Parents push too hard for their kids to be successful at sports.

3. What was Gwen's main problem in this story?

Ⓐ She kicked the ball and missed the net.

Ⓑ She allowed the other team to score.

Ⓒ She did not get along with her teammates.

Ⓓ She felt slow and clumsy.

4. How did Persa help Gwen "find a place for herself" on the team?

_____

_____

5. How did Gwen's feelings about herself change from the beginning of the story to the end?

_____

_____

Name_____ Date_____

Directions: Read the passage. Then use the information from the passage to answer questions 1–5.

The Channel Tunnel

England and France are separated by a body of water. It is called the English Channel. At one time, the only way to cross the channel was by boat. It was a long, slow trip.

In 1802, Napoleon was the ruler of France. He had an idea. He wanted to build a tunnel under the channel. It would connect France and England.

Work began nearly 100 years later. The work was hard. It was very dangerous, too. The project soon ended.

In 1957, people again talked about a tunnel. By then, people could fly from London to Paris. But plane travel was costly. Trains were cheaper. An undersea train seemed like a good idea.

The project cost too much for one country to afford. So England and France worked together. They began in 1973. But they stopped in 1975. The job was too difficult.

In 1987, work began again. Workers started in France and in England. In 1990, the two teams met. They linked the tunnel between England and France!

The first train traveled through the tunnel in 1994. Drivers once had to leave their cars behind. But now they can load them onto a train. The long boat ride has become a 30-minute train ride.

Name _____ Date_____

1. What is the main problem presented in this passage?

(A) Traveling between England and France took a long time.

(B) Napoleon was the ruler of France.

(C) In 1957, people began talking about building a tunnel.

(D) The weather in England was always cold.

2. What problems did the first tunnel builders face?

(A) Only France was interested in the project.

(B) Air travel was much easier.

(C) The project was too hard and dangerous.

(D) The idea of an undersea train was crazy.

3. Most of the details in this passage are presented in what order?

(A) order of importance

(B) time order

(C) size order

(D) alphabetical order

4. How did France and England finally get the tunnel done?

_____

_____

5. How did the tunnel solve a problem for people with cars?

_____

_____

Name_____ Date_____

Directions: Read the passage. Then use the information from the passage to answer questions 1–5.

Comics Then and Now

Do you like to read comics? Most kids do. A lot of adults read comics, too. In fact, the first comics were created for adults.

Let's go back more than 100 years. The year is 1895. You are reading a newspaper called the *New York World*. You see something new in the paper. It has words and pictures. It is called "The Yellow Kid." It is the first newspaper comic. Lots of people enjoy it. So they buy more newspapers.

Jump ahead a few years. It is about 1920. Now other papers have comics, too. One is called "Popeye." Another is called "Krazy Kat." Many people love these comics. The new comics help sell even more newspapers.

A few more years go by. Now the year is 1935. Again you see something new to read. It is the first comic book about a superhero. It is called "Superman." People begin to buy comic books. They love to read about Superman and his great powers.

Today, people still like to read comics. Most comics are funny. They make people laugh. Some comics are serious. They make people think. What kind of comics do you like?

Name _____ Date_____

1. The writer organized the information in this passage by _____.

Ⓐ order of importance

Ⓑ questions and answers

Ⓒ time order

Ⓓ problems and solutions

2. Which comic came first?

Ⓐ "Popeye"

Ⓑ "Krazy Kat"

Ⓒ "Superman"

Ⓓ "The Yellow Kid"

3. Which sentence in the passage helps you understand that "Superman" came out after "Krazy Kat"?

Ⓐ A few more years go by.

Ⓑ Most comics are funny.

Ⓒ It is called "Superman."

Ⓓ Now other papers have comics, too.

4. In what part of the passage can you find out how comics changed in 1935?

_____

_____

5. What does the title tell you about this passage?

_____

_____

Directions: Read the passage. Then use the information from the passage to answer questions 1–5.

Land of Ice and Snow

Our world has seven continents, but Antarctica is quite different from the other six. Antarctica is sometimes called the "White Continent" because it is covered by snow and ice. Antarctica is colder than any other place in the world. It is also windier. It is the only continent that does not have any trees—not a single one!

Sea Creatures

However, that does not mean that Antarctica is empty. In fact, Antarctica has some of the world's largest populations of sea creatures.

The White Continent has nine types of whales and six kinds of seals—more than any of the other continents. Seals live and play on the beaches or on icebergs. They swim in the icy water. Elephant seals are the biggest. Their pups gain about 120 pounds in the first three weeks of life.

Then there are the birds of Antarctica. Thousands of penguins live there. It is the only place in the world where you can see emperor and Adélie penguins in the wild. Another strange and wonderful bird is the albatross. It is one of Earth's biggest birds. Its wingspan can be as wide as twelve feet. This giant bird can fly thousands of miles for food.

Part of Our World

Antarctica includes the South Pole, which is the bottom tip of Earth. Unlike the land on other continents, no country owns Antarctica. Several countries have claimed parts of it. They have set up research stations there. But most countries have agreed to share this unusual place. They will try to keep it clean and pure.

Land of Ice and Snow

Name _____ Date _____

1. **Most of the information in this passage is organized by _____.**
   - Ⓐ time order
   - Ⓑ order of importance
   - Ⓒ problem and solution
   - Ⓓ compare and contrast

2. **In this passage, the purpose of the first paragraph is to _____.**
   - Ⓐ describe the time and place
   - Ⓑ introduce the main idea
   - Ⓒ describe changes in Antarctica
   - Ⓓ give the author's opinion

3. **The information under "Sea Creatures" is presented mainly as _____.**
   - Ⓐ causes and effects
   - Ⓑ problems and solutions
   - Ⓒ categories and examples (descriptions)
   - Ⓓ questions and answers

4. **According to this passage, how is the wildlife in Antarctica different from wildlife on other continents?**

   _____

   _____

5. **In terms of government and politics, how is Antarctica different from the other continents?**

   _____

   _____

Name_____ Date_____

Directions: Read the passage. Then use the information from the passage to answer questions 1–5.

Leonardo da Vinci: Master of Invention

Leonardo da Vinci lived in Italy 500 years ago. You may know him as a great painter. But he was an inventor, too. He filled many notebooks with ideas and drawings for machines. These machines worked with water or air. Some of his machines were built in his lifetime. Many would not be built for hundreds of years. Many are things we use every day.

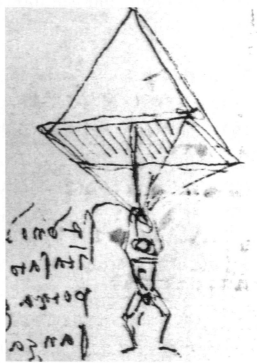

Leonardo was the first to invent a parachute. The parachute helps people float safely from a plane to Earth. Leonardo's was made of stiff linen. It was 36 feet across. Today's parachutes are made of thinner cloth. They are also much smaller. Leonardo's parachute was never made. No one knows if it worked.

Leonardo also created a fan. It was used to move air, just like fans today. But there was no electricity then. Instead, the fan could be turned by hand or by the force of water.

Another of his ideas was a flying ship. Leonardo thought this ship could carry people. It was a small ship with flapping wings. Cranks and screws made the wings move. The wings were supposed to flap like a bat's wings.

Name _____ Date_____

1. How was Leonardo da Vinci's parachute different from parachutes today?

Ⓐ It was much smaller and lighter.

Ⓑ It was bigger and made of a different cloth.

Ⓒ It was very brightly colored.

Ⓓ It had wings that flapped up and down.

2. How were all of Leonardo's machines alike?

Ⓐ They all carried people.

Ⓑ They were all made of cloth.

Ⓒ They were all modeled after animals.

Ⓓ They all worked with water or air.

3. How was Leonardo's fan different from fans used today?

Ⓐ It used electricity.

Ⓑ It did not use electricity.

Ⓒ It was much bigger than fans used today.

Ⓓ It was much smaller than fans used today.

4. How was Leonardo's fan similar to fans used today?

_____

_____

5. How is an airplane similar to Leonardo's flying ship?

_____

_____

Directions: Read the passage. Then use the information from the passage to answer questions 1–5.

A Different Kind of Ride

Do you like to ride your bike? Most people ride bikes in warm weather, but not many ride when it is cold outside. Almost no one rides a bicycle during the snowy winter.

One unusual man does ride on snow, and on ice, too. His name is Doug Stoup. Doug rode his bike in Antarctica! No place on Earth has more ice, snow, wind, and extreme cold.

Of course, Doug has warm clothes, and he has a special bicycle called an ice bike. Like other bikes, Doug's ice bike has two wheels, but the tires are different. They are very fat. Thin tires slip on ice. Fat tires may look funny, but they do not slip as much.

Most bikes have some plastic parts. In very cold weather, plastic can freeze and break. The ice bike has no plastic at all. Antarctica is not a good place for plastic!

In 2003, Doug tested his bike in Antarctica for a week. He rode on ice and snow, and the ice bike worked fine. It did not slip on ice or get stuck in snow. Someday, Doug hopes to ride alone across Antarctica. He wants to go all the way to the South Pole by bike.

Do you think an ice bike sounds like fun? Wait—don't give your old bike away yet! Ice bikes only work well on ice and snow, and they cost about $3,500. But they are no good at all on a warm summer day!

Name _____ Date_____

1. How are ice bikes different from most other bikes?

Ⓐ They cost more money.

Ⓑ They have more wheels.

Ⓒ They are made of plastic.

Ⓓ They are fun to slide on.

2. How are fat tires different from thin tires?

Ⓐ They are better for children's bikes.

Ⓑ They break more easily.

Ⓒ They work better in ice and snow.

Ⓓ They slip and slide a lot more.

3. Riding an ice bike is most similar to _____.

Ⓐ swimming

Ⓑ playing tennis

Ⓒ driving a race car

Ⓓ snowshoeing

4. How is Doug Stoup different from most other people who ride bikes?

_____

_____

5. How is Doug Stoup's bike different from most other bikes?

_____

_____

Name _____ Date _____

Directions: Read the passage. Then use the information from the passage to answer questions 1–5.

Kangaroos and Opossums

Kangaroos and opossums are members of the same animal family. They are alike in many ways, but they are also very different. Both animals are marsupials, so they have pouches. Marsupial mothers carry their babies in these pouches. The babies stay there for up to three months. The mothers can keep them close by and make sure they are safe. They can feed their babies anytime.

They are both warm-blooded animals. (So are people.) Their bodies stay the same temperature all the time. But they live on different sides of the world. Kangaroos come from Australia. Opossums live in the Americas.

Most opossums are about as large as a cat. Kangaroos can be as big as a football player. Some kangaroos are over six feet tall. They can weigh more than 200 pounds.

Kangaroos and opossums both eat plants. But opossums also eat meat. Kangaroos spend their time on the ground and can move around fast. They eat mainly grass. Opossums spend more time in trees. They hang from their tails. This way, they can get food that is hard to reach, but other animals can't get them. Opossums will eat almost anything. They like leaves, fruit, and other plant food. They eat bugs and snails, too.

Kangaroos sleep at night, as most animals do. But opossums come out after dark.

These animals also face danger in different ways. Kangaroos fight by boxing and kicking, but opossums roll up and play dead.

Name _____ Date _____

1. How are kangaroos and opossums alike?
Ⓐ   Both are cold-blooded.
Ⓑ   Both sleep at night.
Ⓒ   Both are marsupials.
Ⓓ   Both come from Australia.

2. How are kangaroos and opossums different?
Ⓐ   Only kangaroos have pouches.
Ⓑ   They are from different animal families.
Ⓒ   They are different sizes.
Ⓓ   Only kangaroos go out at night.

3. How are kangaroos and opossums alike?
Ⓐ   In danger, both box and kick.
Ⓑ   Both come out during the day.
Ⓒ   Both lay eggs in the sand.
Ⓓ   Both carry babies in pouches.

4. How are kangaroos and opossums alike and different in what they eat?

_____

_____

5. How are kangaroos and opossums different in where they usually spend their time?

_____

_____

Directions: Read the passage. Then use the information from the passage to answer questions 1–5.

The Most Exciting Job in the World

Are you curious? Do you like to learn new things? Then you would love my job. I am a space scientist. At work, I ask questions and look for answers. Every day I learn something new. Being a scientist is the most exciting job in the world! It's an important job, too. I can't wait to get to work every day.

My group is studying the planet Saturn. There is so much we need to find out! We want to learn about Saturn's rings. We want to learn about Saturn's dozens of moons. Right now we are studying Titan. Titan is Saturn's biggest moon. Not long ago, we sent a probe that landed on Titan. The probe was about as big as a car. It did a wonderful job. It sent us a lot of information. It also sent pictures.

We thought the probe would work for only a few minutes. But it worked for hours! That was very exciting. Now scientists are studying the information. It will take many years to study it all.

Does that sound like a long time? To a scientist, it is not long at all. We waited a long time to get the information. It took seven years for the probe to reach Titan. A good scientist must be curious. A good scientist must be patient, too!

Name _____ Date_____

1. Which sentence from the passage states a fact?

Ⓐ Then you would love my job.

Ⓑ I am a space scientist.

Ⓒ Being a scientist is the most exciting job in the world!

Ⓓ It's an important job, too.

2. Which sentence from the passage states an opinion?

Ⓐ It took seven years for the probe to reach Titan.

Ⓑ It did a wonderful job.

Ⓒ Now scientists are studying the information.

Ⓓ My group is studying the planet Saturn.

3. Which sentence is an opinion?

Ⓐ The space probe is about the size of a car.

Ⓑ The planet Saturn has dozens of moons.

Ⓒ Saturn is the most interesting planet.

Ⓓ Titan is Saturn's biggest moon.

4. Give one fact and one opinion from the third paragraph.

_____

_____

_____

5. According to the writer of this passage, what makes a good scientist?

_____

_____

_____

Name _____ Date _____

Directions: Read the passage. Then use the information from the passage to answer questions 1–5.

New Video Fun from Giant Games

Get ready for some fun! Buy **Build-A-World** from Giant Games. This is the new video game everyone wants to play. Dads, moms, and kids all love **Build-A-World**. Here are some things players can do with this fun game.

- Make a special place. You can build a town. You can make houses, parks, lakes, and more.

- Create and name characters. You can make a big family or a small one. You can make neighbors, friends, and even pets.

- Make some vehicles. You'll want to travel in your new world. You can make bikes, cars, and trains. You can even make a rocket!

- Play alone or play with others. **Build-A-World** is lots of fun to play alone. It's even more fun to play with others.

Are you a sports nut? You will want **Build-A-Team**. **Build-A-Team** is a ton of fun! Here is what you can do with this game.

- Make a sports team. Pick your sport and give your team a name.

- Pick your players and name them, too.

- Make team uniforms.

- Play to win!

Build-A-World and **Build-A-Team** cost $30.00 each. Or you can buy both great games for only $50.00. Try them both! You'll be glad you did. The whole family will love them!

Giant Games makes games in Chicago, Illinois.

You can buy Giant Games in stores or online.

We send games all over the world.

Name _____ Date_____

1. Which sentence states an opinion?

Ⓐ You can make a sports team with **Build-A-Team**.

Ⓑ It costs $50.00 to buy both video games.

Ⓒ Players can make houses and cars using **Build-A-World**.

Ⓓ **Build-A-World** is lots of fun to play alone.

2. Which sentence from the passage states a fact?

Ⓐ Dads, moms, and kids all love **Build-A-World**.

Ⓑ **Build-A-Team** costs $30.00.

Ⓒ It's even more fun to play with others.

Ⓓ The whole family will love them!

3. Which sentence from the passage states a fact?

Ⓐ You'll be glad you did.

Ⓑ **Build-A-Team** is a ton of fun!

Ⓒ You'll want to travel in your new world.

Ⓓ Giant Games makes games in Chicago, Illinois.

4. Write one sentence from the passage that is a fact and tell why it is a fact.

_____

_____

5. Write one sentence from the passage that states an opinion and tell why it is an opinion.

_____

_____

Directions: Read the passage. Then use the information from the passage to answer questions 1–5.

The Sox and the Bambino

In 1918, the Boston Red Sox won the World Series by beating the Chicago Cubs. One of their stars that year was a young player named Babe Ruth, also known as "The Babe" or "The Bambino." By any name, he was the greatest baseball player of all time.

In 1920, the owner of the Red Sox traded Babe Ruth to the New York Yankees for $100,000. It was the worst trade ever made. The Yankees had never won a World Series, but with Babe Ruth they began winning. Over the next 83 years, they won 26 World Series.

During that time, the Red Sox never won again, and some Sox fans blamed it on the trade. They believed the Babe had put some kind of hex on them. They called it "The Curse of the Bambino."

Of course, nobody really believes in curses. Still, bad things seemed to happen to the Sox at the worst times. Take the 1946 World Series, which came down to the last game. A player on the St. Louis team was coming home with the winning run. The Red Sox second baseman held the ball and the Sox lost. It was not fair that St. Louis won that game.

The same kind of disaster happened in the 1986 World Series against the New York Mets. The Sox were winning, and the game was down to the last out. The ball rolled down to the Red Sox first baseman and went between his legs. The Sox lost again. It was the worst day in the history of baseball.

It looked to be the same story in 2004 when the Sox were playing the Yankees in the playoffs. The Yankees won the first three games, and they were ahead in the fourth game. Many fans may have thought the series was over, but then a wonderful thing happened. The Red Sox tied the game and went on to win in the twelfth inning.

The Red Sox did not lose again that fall. After 86 years, they finally won the World Series, and the "Curse of the Bambino" was put to rest.

Name _____ Date _____

1. Which sentence gives an opinion about Babe Ruth?

Ⓐ   He was also known as "The Babe" or "The Bambino."

Ⓑ   The owner of the Red Sox traded Babe Ruth to the
       New York Yankees.

Ⓒ   With Babe Ruth, the Yankees began winning.

Ⓓ   By any name, he was the greatest baseball player of all time.

2. Which sentence from the passage states a fact?

Ⓐ   It was not fair that St. Louis won that game.

Ⓑ   The "Curse of the Bambino" was put to rest.

Ⓒ   Over the next 83 years, they won 26 World Series.

Ⓓ   It was the worst day in the history of baseball.

3. Which sentence from the passage expresses an opinion?

Ⓐ   Of course, nobody really believes in curses.

Ⓑ   Take the 1946 World Series, which came down to the last game.

Ⓒ   The ball rolled down to the Red Sox first baseman and went
       between his legs.

Ⓓ   The Red Sox did not lose again that fall.

**4. The passage says, "Many fans may have thought the series was
over, but then a wonderful thing happened." Does this sentence
state a fact or an opinion? Tell how you know.**

_____

_____

**5. Write a sentence from the passage and tell whether it states
a fact or an opinion.**

_____

_____

Name _____ Date _____

Directions: Read the passage. Then use the information from the passage to answer questions 1–5.

Growing Up Shawnee

Long ago, the Shawnee lived in the eastern part of what is now the United States. These Native Americans lived together in bands. They hunted, farmed, and gathered wild food. From a young age, Shawnee children learned the skills they needed for this way of life.

A Shawnee baby spent only a few weeks at home with its mother. Then the mother returned to her work. She strapped the baby into a wooden cradle. She wore the cradle on her back as she gathered food or farmed. In about six months, the cradle was set aside. Then the baby could crawl about with other young children while its mother worked. As Shawnee children grew a little older, they learned to help the women with their work.

By the age of nine, Shawnee boys and girls spent most of their time apart. While their fathers hunted deer and bears, boys took hunting lessons from older men. Girls stayed with their mothers and learned different skills. Sewing and cooking lessons took up much of their time. Girls were taught to plant and harvest corn, beans, and other crops. They also learned to tan animal hides and make pots out of clay.

Name _____ Date_____

1. What can you tell about the Shawnee from this passage?

Ⓐ The Shawnee lived on the plains.

Ⓑ Mothers and girls worked hard.

Ⓒ The Shawnee ate only meat and corn.

Ⓓ Fathers made clothes from animal hides.

2. Who taught Shawnee girls the skills they needed to know?

Ⓐ their older sisters

Ⓑ their fathers

Ⓒ their older brothers

Ⓓ their mothers

3. In Shawnee villages, who did most of the hunting?

Ⓐ mothers

Ⓑ older men

Ⓒ fathers

Ⓓ young boys

4. After the age of nine, why did Shawnee boys and girls spend most of their time apart?

_____

_____

5. Write a sentence from the passage that shows that Shawnee girls worked hard.

_____

_____

Name _____ Date _____

Trains of the Future

Have you ever played with magnets? If so, you know that a magnet attracts metal. What happens if you put the same ends of two different magnets together? The poles push away from each other.

An electromagnet works like a magnet does, but it uses electricity. Picture a battery. It has positive and negative ends. Electrons collect on the negative end. When you hook both ends to a wire, electrons rush toward the positive side. This causes a small magnetic field. When you unhook the wire, the electrons stop moving through it.

The newest kind of train works with electromagnets. The train has big magnets under it. The train runs on a track that has electric coils along it. This train is a maglev train.

As the train runs on the track, magnets push and pull it along. This force also lifts the train. The train rises up, or levitates, an inch or two above the track. It doesn't touch the track at all. This lets it run at super speeds.

Germany, Japan, and China have made maglev trains. The trains run at more than half the speed of a plane. A maglev train could run from one coast of the United States to the other in about ten hours.

Right now, maglev trains are expensive. Some people think they are not practical. But that may change. The cost may come down. If so, maglev trains may become the trains of the future.

Name _____ Date_____

1. **What happens when the wire that connects both ends of a battery is unhooked?**
   Ⓐ The magnetic field disappears.
   Ⓑ The battery attracts metal.
   Ⓒ The magnetic field increases.
   Ⓓ The electrons fall out of the battery.

2. **Based on the passage, what is true of trains that run on tracks?**
   Ⓐ They cross the United States in ten hours.
   Ⓑ They are not used any longer in China or Japan.
   Ⓒ They cannot run as fast as maglev trains.
   Ⓓ They cost nearly as much as maglev trains.

3. **From this passage, what can you conclude about Germany, Japan, and China?**
   Ⓐ They use trains more than cars and trucks.
   Ⓑ They do not have room for more trains.
   Ⓒ They have spent a lot of money on maglev trains.
   Ⓓ They will not sell their trains.

4. **Which clues from the passage tell you that most countries will not have maglev trains for a long time?**

   _____

   _____

5. **How can a maglev train run above the track and not on the track? Use details from the passage to explain.**

   _____

   _____

Directions: Read the passage. Then use the information from the passage to answer questions 1–5.

Pests

A pest is a plant or animal that does not live naturally in an area but somehow ends up there. Sometimes a new species arrives by accident. Sometimes it is brought to a place on purpose. These new plants and animals can cause serious problems.

At one time there were no rabbits in Australia. A man named Thomas Austin took twenty-four rabbits there in 1859. Seven years later, the number of rabbits had really grown. One of Austin's neighbors killed more than two million rabbits on his land. People called the rabbits the "gray blanket." The rabbits ate crops and left fields bare. People put up fences, but the rabbits climbed them. People shot the rabbits and used poison to kill them. At last, the rabbits were under control.

Similar events have happened in the United States. Zebra mussels were first found in 1988. By 1990, they had spread to all the Great Lakes. Today, zebra mussels can be found in more than 20 states.

Zebra mussels stop the flow of water through pipes. They ruin docks. They attach themselves to boats and prevent the boats from running. They also kill other shellfish. Because the mussels eat the same food as some other shellfish and there are so many of them, the other shellfish run out of food.

New species travel to other countries all the time. Plant seeds can enter a country easily. They can even arrive on the bottom of a person's shoe. Some animals enter as pets. Insects can come in on airplanes, cars, or ships. People have to be careful about bringing plants and animals to different areas. Introducing a new species often does more harm than good.

Name _____ Date _____

1. What conclusion about rabbits can be drawn from this passage?

Ⓐ They are very fierce.

Ⓑ They are hard to kill.

Ⓒ They kill other animals.

Ⓓ Their numbers grow very quickly.

2. What evidence supports your conclusion?

Ⓐ At one time there were no rabbits in Australia.

Ⓑ A neighbor of Austin's killed over two million rabbits.

Ⓒ The rabbits could climb fences.

Ⓓ The rabbits came from England.

3. What can you conclude from the description of the rabbits as a "gray blanket"?

Ⓐ They are used to make blankets.

Ⓑ They are very soft.

Ⓒ They cover the ground like a blanket.

Ⓓ There are not many rabbits.

4. What can you conclude from this passage about where zebra mussels came from?

_____

_____

5. What evidence supports the conclusion that keeping a new species out of the country is very hard?

_____

_____

Directions: Read the passage. Then use the information from the passage to answer questions 1–5.

A Sweet Time of Year

In parts of New England, the snow in the woods begins to melt in March. When the sun gets warm enough, something special happens. The sap in the maple trees starts to run! It flows from the roots up through the trees. This is the time to make maple syrup. If you eat pancakes with real maple syrup, you know how sweet that syrup tastes!

In New England, many people make maple syrup. There are several steps in making it. First, you have to tap the tree. This means that you drill a hole in the trunk of a sugar maple tree. Then you put in a tap or a tube. The sap flows from the tree into a bucket. When the bucket is full, workers pour the sap into a big vat. The vat is used to boil the sap over a fire.

As it boils, the sap gets thicker. Before long, most of the water has boiled off. What is left is good, thick syrup. It smells wonderful, and it tastes great. Some makers like to pour hot maple syrup on homemade doughnuts and eat them as they work. Others make maple sugar candy.

To make one gallon of syrup takes 40 to 60 gallons of sap. Making syrup is hard work. But syrup makers love this time of year. The season only lasts about three weeks, and making syrup is fun. When the trees begin to bud, the season ends.

In the United States, Vermont makes more maple syrup than any other state. It produces about 400,000 gallons of syrup every year. New York makes about 200,000 gallons. Several other states make syrup, too.

Name _____ Date_____

1. This passage was written mainly to _____.
- Ⓐ tell how maple syrup is made
- Ⓑ give information about Vermont
- Ⓒ tell how to cook pancakes
- Ⓓ make people plant more trees

2. The author probably mentioned pancakes in this passage because he wanted to suggest that _____.
- Ⓐ pancakes are good for you
- Ⓑ many people like maple syrup
- Ⓒ pancakes are easy to make
- Ⓓ eating breakfast is important

3. The author probably mentioned Vermont and New York in this passage to _____.
- Ⓐ make people want to visit those states
- Ⓑ tell how much maple syrup costs
- Ⓒ describe how people eat maple syrup
- Ⓓ tell where maple syrup is made

4. What does the author think of maple syrup season? Give a detail from the passage to support your answer.

_____

_____

5. What is the author's opinion of maple syrup? Give a detail from the passage to support your answer.

_____

_____

Directions: *Read the passage. Then use the information from the passage to answer questions 1–5.*

From the Police Chief's Mailbag

Dear Chief Norman,

I have lived in town all of my life. I went to Elmwood Elementary School for six years. At first I walked to school with my brother. When we were older, we rode our bikes to school. We both loved that!

Now I am a parent, and my children go to Elmwood School. They often beg me to let them ride bikes to school. Chief Norman, I want them to ride. I wish they could! But today there are so many cars in town. There is much more traffic than in the past. To get to school, Tim and Tonya must cross Great Plain Road. They cannot cross this busy street alone. No child can. A police officer could help children cross safely. I have talked with many parents in my neighborhood. We need your help. Our children need your help.

You can help in one of these ways. Hire a crossing guard to help children cross. Or send a police officer to help the children. I know the police work hard to keep people safe. This is a way to keep our children safe.

My number is 555-1530. I will wait for your call. Thank you for reading my letter.

Yours truly,

Lily Cho

Name _____ Date_____

1. Lily Cho wrote this letter because she wanted to _____ .
Ⓐ get a job as a crossing guard
Ⓑ thank the police chief for his work
Ⓒ get someone to help children cross a busy street
Ⓓ tell people she had lived in town all her life

2. Why does Mrs. Cho think that police should help children cross the street?
Ⓐ It is part of their job of keeping people safe.
Ⓑ No one else can do it
Ⓒ She loved to ride her bike to school when she was a child.
Ⓓ The parents are all too busy.

3. Lily Cho hopes that Chief Norman will _____ .
Ⓐ lower the speed limit for drivers
Ⓑ make it safe for children to ride to school
Ⓒ cut down on the traffic in town
Ⓓ teach children how to cross streets safely

4. Why did Mrs. Cho include her telephone number in the letter?

_____

_____

5. How does Mrs. Cho feel about children riding bikes to school?

_____

_____

Name _____ Date _____

Directions: Read the passage. Then use the information from the passage to answer questions 1–5.

Living on a Kibbutz

Beginning in the late 1800s, many Jews left Russia seeking freedom. They went to Palestine. That was the homeland of the Jewish people from long ago. The Jews from Russia were poor but full of hope.

In 1909, some young Jews started a farm at a place called Degania. It was next to the Sea of Galilee. They owned and worked the land together. They decided things as a group. They all took care of one another. Degania became the first kibbutz, or group-owned farm. At first, only adults lived on the kibbutz. They cleared the land and planted crops.

Over the next few decades, the kibbutz movement grew in Palestine. Children were born. Schools had to be built. Because all adults were equal, both men and women worked in the fields. This meant that day-care centers were built for the young children. All children slept together in children's houses.

On the kibbutz, everyone acted like one big family. People ate together. They took hikes and played music together. It was a wonderful way of life!

Today, there are over 250 kibbutzim in Israel. Although the basic beliefs are the same, life on a kibbutz today is sadly much different from in the past. Children live at home with their parents. Most families stay at home for entertainment rather than do things, like folk dancing, with the rest of the group. Farming is no longer the most important thing on a kibbutz.

In the old days, everyone on a kibbutz was equal. Today, the sense of being equal has been lost.

Progress-Monitoring Comprehension Strategy Assessments ❹

Name _____ Date _____

1. **The author of this passage told about the Jews who left Russia because he wanted to _____.**
   Ⓐ compare Russia with Palestine
   Ⓑ explain how Palestine became Israel
   Ⓒ describe their farms in Russia
   Ⓓ explain how the first kibbutz began

2. **The author's main purpose in writing this passage was to _____.**
   Ⓐ describe the sights and sounds of a kibbutz
   Ⓓ give a brief history of the kibbutz
   Ⓒ persuade people to live on a kibbutz
   Ⓓ tell a made-up story about a child on a kibbutz

3. **At the end of the passage, the author gives information about life on a kibbutz today to show that _____.**
   Ⓐ all the people still do everything together
   Ⓑ everyone who lives on a kibbutz is happy
   Ⓒ things have changed a lot since the first kibbutz
   Ⓓ the people of Israel are very friendly

4. **How does the author of this passage seem to feel about having the children on a kibbutz sleep together in children's houses? Give a detail from the passage to support your answer.**

   _____

   _____

5. **Write a clue from the passage that suggests that the author thinks that the old way of life on a kibbutz was better than the new way.**

   _____

   _____

Name_____ Date _____

Directions: Read the passage. Then use the information from the passage to answer questions 1–5.

The Tundra

The Arctic tundra is near the North Pole. It is the coldest biome, or habitat, in the world. The layer of soil below the surface is always frozen. There are no trees. The temperature ranges from 20°F to minus 70°F. The growing season lasts only 50 to 60 days. This is why the biome has little plant life. Grass, moss, and sedge grow here.

Several kinds of animals live in the tundra. Some, like reindeer and rabbits, eat plants. Others, like polar bears and wolves, eat meat. They hunt the plant-eating animals. The Arctic tundra is home to some insects and birds as well.

The Arctic tundra is changing. People are causing the changes. They drive snowmobiles and cars into the area. They run over the plants. It takes many years for the plants to grow back. Meanwhile, many animals lack food. Their numbers are getting smaller.

People are also hunting in the tundra. They are killing seals, polar bears, and reindeer. But laws are being passed to limit the hunting of animals.

As you can see, tundra wildlife is fragile. People must take care of this habitat. If they don't, many species of plants and animals could become extinct.

Name _____ Date_____

1. What causes the tundra to have little plant life?

Ⓐ   There are no trees.   Ⓑ   The growing season is short.

Ⓒ   Rabbits and bears live there.   Ⓓ   People drive snowmobiles.

2. What is the effect of plant life being destroyed?

Ⓐ   Animals do not have enough food to eat.

Ⓑ   People drive snowmobiles into this ecosystem.

Ⓒ   Moss grows in the tundra.

Ⓓ   The temperature drops to between 20°F and minus 70°F.

3. What will happen if people do not take care of the tundra habitat?

Ⓐ   Polar bears and wolves will hunt the plant-eating animals.

Ⓑ   The growing season will last only 50 to 60 days.

Ⓒ   Cars and snowmobiles will break down in the tundra.

Ⓓ   Many plants and animals will become extinct.

4. Why is the Arctic tundra changing? Give two reasons found in the passage.

_____

_____

5. What effect does driving snowmobiles have on the tundra?

_____

_____

Directions: Read the passage. Then use the information from the passage to answer questions 1–5.

Helping Some Big Babies

Is there a baby in your family? Then you know babies need lots of care. They cannot take care of themselves when they are little.

Elephant babies are not little. Still, they need lots of care. They cannot take care of themselves. That's why Daphne Sheldrick started an orphanage in Africa. It is an orphanage for elephants! Daphne lives in Kenya near Tsavo National Park. She runs the orphanage at her home.

Zoe is a young elephant. When Zoe came to the orphanage, she was just two weeks old. Zoe was hungry. She needed good food and good care. Zoe lived at the orphanage for a year. She got bigger and stronger. Then workers took her to the park. There they help Zoe learn to find her own food. They keep her in a safe, fenced-in place at night. Someday Zoe will go and live in the wild. Workers will know when she is ready to go.

Why are there orphans like Zoe? Sometimes adult elephants go onto farms and harm plants. Farmers kill some of the elephants. Hunters kill even more. They sell the elephants' ivory. People make things from ivory.

Daphne wants people to stop using ivory. Then no one would buy it from the hunters. Maybe there would be no more need for the elephant orphanage.

Name _____ Date_____

1. Why did Daphne Sheldrick start an orphanage for elephants?

Ⓐ She lives near a park.

Ⓑ Elephant babies cannot take care of themselves.

Ⓒ She likes all kinds of animals.

Ⓓ Zoe was just two weeks old, and she was hungry.

2. Farmers in Africa sometimes kill elephants because _____.

Ⓐ they like to hunt

Ⓑ they want to make things from ivory

Ⓒ the elephants hurt plants

Ⓓ the elephants need lots of care

3. For Zoe, what was the effect of living at the orphanage?

Ⓐ She went to live in the wild.

Ⓑ She got bigger and stronger.

Ⓒ A hunter wanted her ivory.

Ⓓ She was lost and hungry.

4. Why are there orphan elephants in Africa? Give two reasons found in the passage.

_____

_____

5. If no one used ivory anymore, what would probably happen to elephants?

_____

_____

Directions: Read the passage. Then use the information from the passage to answer questions 1–5.

Sailing to California

In the 1850s, the trip west to California was long and hard. It could take months. People traveled in heavy covered wagons. They carried food for the long trip as well as clothes and other supplies. Most of the wagons were pulled by oxen, horses, or mules, but the animals had trouble pulling the wagons uphill and downhill. The animals got very tired, and some even died on the trip.

Zeb Thomas thought long and hard about this problem. Thomas wanted to find a way to travel across the prairie without using animals. He knew the prairies were flat and windy. He wanted to build a special wagon with a sail so the wind would push it along the ground. Thomas hoped that his idea would work and would make him rich.

Zeb Thomas became known as "Windwagon" Thomas. He found several investors who gave him money to help him build his wagon. These people hoped the windwagon would make them rich, too.

Windwagon Thomas got his wagon ready for its first trip. It was twenty-five feet long and seven feet wide with wheels over ten feet high. In the center of the wagon was a seven-foot mast with a sail.

People crowded around to watch the wagon's first trip. The sail picked up the wind, and the wagon started to roll. The windwagon worked! When the wind grew stronger, the wagon went faster. Then the trail dipped down the side of a hill. The wagon, moving at a very high speed, smashed into the side of the hill. It was crushed.

Thomas crawled out of the wreck. He wasn't hurt, but his investors were so angry that they ran him out of town. That was the last time anyone tried to build a windwagon.

Name _____ Date _____

1. Why was the trip to California so difficult for oxen, horses, and mules?

Ⓐ They were not fed properly.

Ⓑ Most of the land was flat.

Ⓒ They had to pull heavy wagons.

Ⓓ The wind blew all the time.

2. Why did Windwagon Thomas want his wagon to work?

Ⓐ He wanted to be famous.

Ⓑ He thought it would make him rich.

Ⓒ He had made a bet with someone about it.

Ⓓ It was his greatest dream.

3. What was the result of the windwagon's first trip?

Ⓐ The wagon worked beautifully.

Ⓑ The animals got tired.

Ⓒ The investors gave Thomas money.

Ⓓ The wagon crashed.

4. What caused the wagon to crash?

_____

_____

5. How did the windwagon's crash affect the investors? Tell what they did.

_____

_____

Name _____ Date _____

Directions: Read the passage. Then use the information from the passage to answer questions 1–5.

The Great Pyramid

The Great Pyramid was built by King Khufu in Egypt. Only a few things are known about him. He lived around 2500 B.C. He ruled for about 20 years. Some people believe that he was a bad ruler. They think he made his people build the pyramid. No one knows if this is true.

The Great Pyramid rises 449 feet above the plain at Giza. It is the largest pyramid. The base of the pyramid is huge. It covers seven city blocks. Each side of the base is 754 feet long.

Early visitors stole nearly everything from the Great Pyramid. When scientists found it in the 1800s, the beautiful decorations were gone. One thing was found nearby. It was a large, wooden boat called the Sun Boat. The Egyptians thought the boat would carry Khufu into the next life.

The Great Pyramid is not as great as it once was. When it was built, it was 30 feet higher than it is now. Time and weather have worn it down. Still, it is an amazing thing to see.

Name _____ Date_____

1. What is the stated main idea in this passage?

Ⓐ The Great Pyramid was built by King Khufu of Egypt.

Ⓑ Early visitors stole nearly everything from the Great Pyramid.

Ⓒ King Khufu made his people build a pyramid.

Ⓓ Blocks of stone were used to build the pyramid.

2. Which detail supports the main idea in paragraph two that the Great Pyramid is very tall?

Ⓐ Its base is as large as seven city blocks.

Ⓑ It is the largest pyramid.

Ⓒ It rises 449 feet above the plain at Giza.

Ⓓ It covers seven city blocks.

3. What is the stated main idea in the last paragraph?

Ⓐ Time and weather have worn down the Great Pyramid.

Ⓑ The Great Pyramid is not as great as it once was.

Ⓒ The Great Pyramid is an amazing thing to see.

Ⓓ The Great Pyramid was once 30 feet higher.

4. What is the stated main idea in paragraph three?

_____

_____

5. What details support the idea that few things are known about King Khufu?

_____

_____

Directions: Read the passage. Then use the information from the passage to answer questions 1–5.

Become a Cloud Watcher

Look up at the sky. Most likely, you will see clouds. All clouds are made of water, snow, or ice. But not all clouds are the same. If you learn about clouds, you can tell a lot about the weather. Here are some kinds of clouds you are likely to see.

On fair, sunny days you may see cumulus clouds. These clouds are fat and puffy. They look like soft cotton floating in the sky. When you see cumulus clouds, the weather will stay fair.

Cumulonimbus clouds are bigger and much taller. If you see these dark clouds, watch out. They bring bad weather. They will surely bring rain or hail. They often bring thunder and lightning. Sometimes they bring dangerous storms called tornadoes.

Some clouds are quite low in the sky. They are called stratus clouds. These low clouds may even hide the tops of tall buildings. When you see stratus clouds, expect some light rain. In the winter, stratus clouds may bring snow.

Cirrus clouds are thin and wispy. These pretty clouds are very high in the sky. They are made of tiny bits of ice. It is fun to watch them move, curl and change shape. Look for cirrus clouds when the weather is fair.

Become a cloud watcher. Notice each cloud's shape and size. Then you will know what kind of cloud it is. You will know what kind of weather to expect. Best of all, you will not miss the beauty of the clouds in the sky.

Name _____ Date_____

1. What is this passage mostly about?
Ⓐ different kinds of clouds   Ⓑ learning about science
Ⓒ sunny days and rainy days   Ⓓ how clouds are made

2. What is the main idea in paragraph one?
Ⓐ More people should look at the sky every day and see the clouds.
Ⓑ If you look up, you will always see clouds.
Ⓒ There are different kinds of clouds, and they tell about the weather.
Ⓓ Clouds are made of water, snow, or ice.

3. Which sentence best states the main idea of this passage?
Ⓐ Certain kinds of clouds are sure to bring rain.
Ⓑ You should know what kind of weather to expect.
Ⓒ Some clouds are better and prettier than others.
Ⓓ It is enjoyable and worthwhile to be a cloud watcher.

4. Give three details from the passage to support the idea that you should watch out when you see cumulonimbus clouds.

_____

_____

_____

_____

5. What would be another good title for this passage?

_____

_____

Directions: Read the passage. Then use the information from the passage to answer questions 1–5.

The Lost Colony

In the 1600s, many people from England sailed to America. They wanted to build new towns and start new lives. The first permanent English settlement was Jamestown. It was founded in Virginia in 1607. The Pilgrims founded Plymouth in 1620. There was another colony before either of these two, but it disappeared.

In 1585, Sir Walter Raleigh sent 108 men to America. They landed on Roanoke Island. That is off the coast of what is now North Carolina. A year later they were starving. So they returned to England.

In 1587, Raleigh sent another group of settlers to Roanoke. There were 117 men, women, and children. The leader was a man named John White. His daughter was Eleanor Dare. She had a baby soon after the group arrived. The baby was named Virginia Dare. She was the first English child born in America.

After only a week at Roanoke, John White sailed back to England. He had to get more tools and supplies. But England went to war with Spain soon after that. So White stayed in England for almost three years.

When John White finally returned to Roanoke in 1590, the people were gone. The only clue left behind was the word *Croatoan*. It was carved into a post. Croatoan was the name of a nearby island. So White thought the people had moved to a better place. However, none of the colonists was ever seen again. To this day, no one knows what happened to them.

Name _____ Date _____

1. What is this passage mostly about?
Ⓐ   the colony of Jamestown, Virginia
Ⓑ   the birth of a child named Virginia Dare
Ⓒ   a colony in America that disappeared
Ⓓ   the war between England and Spain

2. According to the passage, where was the first English settlement in America?
Ⓐ   Jamestown
Ⓑ   Croatoan
Ⓒ   Plymouth
Ⓓ   Roanoke Island

3. In one sentence, write the main idea of the third paragraph in your own words.

_____

_____

4. Which detail supports the idea that the people of the Roanoke colony had planned to move to another place?
Ⓐ   John White remained in England.
Ⓑ   The word *Croatoan* was carved into a post.
Ⓒ   England went to war with Spain.
Ⓓ   The first English child was born at Roanoke.

5. Write a detail from the passage supporting the idea that John White stayed in England too long before he returned to Roanoke.

_____

_____

Name _____ Date _____

Directions: Read the passage. Then use the information from the passage to answer questions 1–5.

Making a Budget

A budget is a plan for getting, spending, and saving money. Follow these steps to make a budget.

First, get a notebook. Each page will be for a different week. Write the date at the top of the page. Then draw and label a chart as shown below.

In the first box, write down all the money you expect to get: exactly how much it will be and where it will come from. In the second box, write down where this money will go. Start with all necessary expenses. Then write down things you would like to spend money on. Last, write down how much money you plan to save, if any.

This is your plan, which may or may not work out. Keep track of what really happens in the boxes on the right.

Budgets are a great way to track your money. If you get into the habit of keeping a budget now, you will learn to manage your money for the future.

What I Planned	**What Really Happened**
MONEY IN—PLANNED	MONEY IN—REAL
Allowance $5	Allowance $5
Money for yard work $3	Money for yard work . . . . . $0 (rained)
Birthday money $15	Birthday money $10
Total $23	**Total** $15
MONEY OUT—PLANNED	MONEY OUT—REAL
Present for Grandma $10	Present for Grandma $12
Snack at pool $3	Savings $3
Savings $10	
Total $23	**Total** $15

Name _____ Date_____

1. What should you do first to make a budget?

Ⓐ Draw a chart.   Ⓑ Write the date.

Ⓒ Get a notebook.   Ⓓ Label the chart.

2. After you make a chart for your budget, what should you do next?

Ⓐ Write the date on each page.

Ⓑ Make a list of things you want to buy.

Ⓒ Estimate how much money you can save each week.

Ⓓ Write the amount of money you expect to get.

3. What will happen if you take in more money than you spend?

Ⓐ You will need a new notebook.

Ⓑ You will have money left over.

Ⓒ You will become rich.

Ⓓ You will make some new friends.

4. When you make your budget, what is the first thing you should write in the box for MONEY OUT — PLANNED?

_____

_____

5. With this kind of budget, what should you do at the end of each week?

_____

_____

Name _____ Date _____

All Mixed Up

Water is a clear, colorless, action-packed liquid. Perform this experiment to see for yourself.

What You Need:
small jar filled with water
red and yellow food coloring

What You Do:
1. Set the jar in a place where you can leave it for several hours.

2. Add two drops of red food coloring and two drops of yellow food coloring to the water. Notice how the food coloring sinks to the bottom of the jar.

3. Check the jar in three or four hours to see how the water has changed.

What Happens:
You will find a jar of orange water!

Why It Happens:
Food coloring is heavier than water, so it sinks to the bottom of the jar when first added. Water is made up of tiny particles that are always moving. As these particles bounce around in the jar, they cause the food-coloring particles to mix together.

After you have done the experiment, be sure to clean up properly.

Name _____ Date_____

1. Which step comes first?

Ⓐ   Put red food coloring in the jar.

Ⓑ   Check the jar in three hours.

Ⓒ   Set the jar in its chosen place.

Ⓓ   Put yellow food coloring in the jar.

2. Just after you add the red food coloring, what happens to it?

Ⓐ   It turns orange.

Ⓑ   It mixes with the yellow food coloring.

Ⓒ   It starts to move upward.

Ⓓ   It sinks to the bottom of the jar.

3. What should you do three or four hours after you start the experiment?

Ⓐ   Check to see how the water has changed.

Ⓑ   Move the jar to a different place.

Ⓒ   Stir the food coloring and water together.

Ⓓ   Add some drops of orange food coloring.

4. What happens in the jar after the food coloring sinks?

_____

_____

5. What should you do after the water in the jar turns orange?

_____

_____

Name _____ Date _____

Directions: Read the passage. Then use the information from the passage to answer questions 1–5.

A Long Journey

The monarch butterflies of North America do something no other butterflies do. When fall comes, they leave their homes in the northern United States and Canada. They travel 3,000 miles to spend the winter in California or Mexico. They travel north again in the spring.

Monarch butterfly eggs hatch in the late summer. First, the butterflies gain energy by drinking nectar from flowers. Then they begin the trip south. The butterflies can fly at speeds of up to twelve miles an hour. They also glide on the air to save energy.

Monarch butterflies travel in large groups. They face many dangers during the journey. Storms can push them off course or kill them. Many die when they fly into moving trucks and cars. Others are eaten by birds. Some just get too tired to finish the trip. Still, a large number of butterflies finish the trip. In one part of Mexico, up to 300 million monarchs spend the winter.

In late February, the butterflies begin to move north again. They lay eggs along the way. New butterflies hatch and continue the trip. Finally, these new butterflies reach their summer homes.

Scientists wonder how monarch butterflies know where to go in the fall and spring. No butterfly ever lives long enough to make the trip more than once. Yet they always return to the same places. What tells them where to go? Scientists hope to learn the answer to this puzzle someday.

Progress-Monitoring Comprehension Strategy Assessments ❹

Name _____ Date _____

1. What do monarch butterflies do first to get ready for their trip south?

Ⓐ They rest for the winter.

Ⓑ They lay eggs.

Ⓒ They fly on air currents.

Ⓓ They drink nectar for energy.

2. What happens last on the trip north?

Ⓐ The monarchs are eaten by birds.

Ⓑ The monarchs reach their summer homes.

Ⓒ The monarchs lay eggs.

Ⓓ The monarchs drink nectar.

3. What do these butterflies do when fall comes?

Ⓐ They begin to fly south.

Ⓑ They lay eggs.

Ⓒ They begin to fly north.

Ⓓ They arrive at their summer homes.

4. According to the passage, what happens in late February?

_____

_____

5. Write two sentences using signal words to describe what the butterflies do after they begin their trip north.

_____

_____

Directions: Read the passage. Then use the information from the passage to answer questions 1–5.

Just Not Herself

The phone call came the day after Hank put up the posters. "Your cat's in my yard," a woman's voice said. "Please come get her right now!"

"Is she a gray-and-brown tiger with white paws?" Hank asked anxiously.

"Just like the cat in the poster!" the woman snapped. "Come get her!"

Hank ran two blocks to the woman's house. He picked up the crouching Snowshoes and said, "She must be starving after being lost for three days."

But at home, Snowshoes ignored her cat food. That night, instead of sleeping on Hank's bed, Snowshoes howled at the door. Finally, Hank let her out. "Snowshoes is just not herself," he decided.

The next day, Dr. Ward examined Snowshoes and told Hank not to worry. But Hank was not convinced.

When Hank got home, his mother met him at the door. "We're going to bring that cat to the animal shelter," she said. "They'll find a home for her."

"Mom!" cried Hank. "Dr. Ward said she'll be herself in a few days. Please don't make me give her up!"

Mom laughed and said, "The real Snowshoes came home while you were gone. She's on her third can of cat food and is purring away!"

Name _____ Date_____

1. How did the woman feel about the cat in her yard?

Ⓐ She thought the cat was beautiful.

Ⓑ She disliked the cat.

Ⓒ She wanted to keep the cat.

Ⓓ She felt sorry for the cat.

2. When Hank brought Snowshoes home, the cat seemed _____.

Ⓐ frisky   Ⓑ hungry

Ⓒ tired   Ⓓ unfriendly

3. Dr. Ward is the kind of doctor who _____.

Ⓐ takes care of animals

Ⓑ visits people in their homes

Ⓒ sets people's broken bones

Ⓓ works only with young children

4. Name two kinds of information that were given in Hank's poster.

_____

_____

5. Why do you think Hank named his cat Snowshoes?

_____

_____

Name _____ Date _____

Directions: *Read the passage. Then use the information from the passage to answer questions 1–5.*

Harriet the Tortoise

Every November 15, the Australia Zoo had a birthday party for a tortoise named Harriet. She was the oldest known living creature on Earth.

Harriet was born about 1830. She lived in the Galápagos Islands. When she was about five years old, Harriet was taken to England. Twelve years later, she was moved to a zoo in Australia. For more than 100 years, visitors rode on Harriet's back. Some even carved their name into her shell.

In 1988, Harriet moved to a new home. There, visitors were not allowed to touch her. They could not ride on her back. Only zookeepers and workers could touch her.

Harriet lived in comfort. She was fed a healthful diet of plants. The enclosure she lived in had grass, shady trees, and a small pool. It also had a special cave where she could stay cool on warm days.

Other animals at the zoo were more exciting than Harriet. But when visitors found out her age, they fell in love with her. And every November 15, they sang "Happy Birthday" to her. Harriet died in 2006. She was 176 years old.

Name _____ Date_____

1. **What can you infer from this passage about Harriet in her home in Australia?**
   Ⓐ The people at the zoo cared about Harriet.
   Ⓑ Visitors to the zoo enjoyed feeding Harriet.
   Ⓒ Harriet liked to eat bugs and small animals.
   Ⓓ Harriet lived on an island in the ocean.

2. **Which clue from the passage supports the inference that people are impressed by something that is old?**
   Ⓐ Every November, the Australia Zoo had a birthday party.
   Ⓑ Harriet was born about 1830.
   Ⓒ Other animals at the zoo were more exciting than Harriet.
   Ⓓ When visitors found out her age, they fell in love with her.

3. **Which inference can be made about Harriet's life at the Australia Zoo?**
   Ⓐ She enjoyed the birthday parties the zoo gave her.
   Ⓑ She was more protected than she was in the past.
   Ⓒ She did not mind giving rides to zoo visitors.
   Ⓓ She had to find her own food there.

4. **Which clues from the passage support the inference that Harriet lived a healthy life?**

   _____

   _____

5. **What is the most likely reason that visitors were not allowed to ride on Harriet anymore?**

   _____

   _____

Name _____ Date _____

Directions: Read the passage. Then use the information from the passage to answer questions 1–5.

Mapping the Pacific

In the mid-1700s, Europeans knew very little about the Pacific Ocean. Almost no one had been there. They thought there might be a continent in the South Pacific. If there was, England wanted it. But who would make such a long, hard trip to find out?

Captain James Cook was just the man. His dream was to travel farther than any man had ever been.

Captain Cook came from a poor family. He was a smart and curious boy who learned quickly. When he started working on ships, his interest in math helped him become a great navigator. Then he joined the British Navy and became a maker of maps. His maps of Canada's St. Lawrence River were used into the early 1900s.

From 1768 to 1779, Captain Cook sailed around the world three times for England. Each trip took three or four years. He explored New Zealand and Australia. He found many islands, such as Hawaii. Scientists then thought there might be land at the South Pole. He sailed close to Antarctica three times but was too far away to see it. Ice always forced him to turn back. Still, he sailed farther south than any other explorer.

Captain Cook also made history by keeping his men alive. At the time, sailors ate mostly salted meat and bread crawling with bugs. No wonder so many of them became ill and often died! He gave his men fresh fruit and vegetables. This kept them from getting sick on long ocean trips.

The great Captain James Cook did travel farther than any man had ever been. He went as far as it was possible to go.

Name _____ Date _____

1. From the passage, what can you infer about Captain Cook?

Ⓐ   He was very brave.

Ⓑ   He was a fool to take such risks.

Ⓒ   He was spoiled as a child.

Ⓓ   He was afraid of ice.

2. You can infer from the passage that a navigator is a person who _____.

Ⓐ   travels a lot

Ⓑ   comes from a poor family

Ⓒ   learns quickly

Ⓓ   guides a ship from place to place

3. From the information in this passage, what can you infer about Cook's maps of Canada?

Ⓐ   There was no money to make new maps.

Ⓑ   His maps were quite accurate.

Ⓒ   Not many ship captains used his maps.

Ⓓ   Cook was a skilled artist.

4. Why didn't most sailors in the 1700s eat more fruits and vegetables?

_____

_____

5. Write one or two clues from the passage suggesting that most people of the 1700s did not know much about the rest of the world.

_____

_____

Directions: Read the passage. Then use the information from the passage to answer questions 1–5.

She Says, He Says

Dear Diary,

Help! Mom and Mrs. Newman made plans to spend tomorrow at the beach. That means I have to spend the day with Bennie Newman, and that means he's going to realize that I can't swim!

I know what will happen. When I put on my life jacket, Bennie's going to smirk and say, "Looks like Brainy Janey flunked swimming class!" Then he's going to spread the word to all his cool friends, and they'll tease me, too.

Mom says I'm being silly. "Lots of kids your age are still learning how to swim," she told me. "If Bennie has a problem with that, just ignore him."

Okay, Mom, I can tell it's been a long time since you've embarrassed yourself in front of the coolest kid in school.

Dear Diary,

I can see it now. Janey Ames is going to swim out to the raft and then wave and yell, "The water's great, Bennie! Why don't you come in?"

So I'll wade in and do my ridiculous doggie paddle, and she'll laugh her head off. In a few days, all her brainy friends will know that I can't swim.

So I guess I'll just try to fool her. I'll bring all my sand toys to the beach and start building a sand castle, and I'll casually tell Janey I'd rather build than swim. Of course, she'll probably start building her own castle, and she'll make it bigger and better than mine.

It's going to be a completely awful day!

Name _____ Date_____

1. From reading the first part of the passage, what can you predict about the next day?

Ⓐ Bennie and Janey will take swimming lessons together.

Ⓑ Janey will forget her life jacket.

Ⓒ Bennie and Janey will meet at the beach.

Ⓓ Janey will save Bennie from drowning.

2. How will Janey feel when she first sees Bennie at the beach?

Ⓐ embarrassed   Ⓑ afraid

Ⓒ confident   Ⓓ sad

3. How will Bennie probably feel when he learns Janey's secret?

Ⓐ sorry   Ⓑ upset

Ⓒ amused   Ⓓ relieved

4. What will Bennie most likely bring with him?

_____

5. What will Bennie and Janey find out about each other?

_____

_____

Name _____ Date _____

Directions: Read the passage. Then use the information from the passage to answer questions 1–5.

Giving Robots a Sense of Touch

Many robots can move and "see" with light sensors. Today, scientists want to help robots "feel."

Scientists have made a robot finger out of a special kind of plastic. This plastic can sense changes in pressure or electrical current. The robot finger can sense the weight of an object. It can change its grip to fit the object, too. If the object is heavy, the finger holds it tightly. If it is light, the finger holds it gently.

Engineers are working on robots with a sense of touch. One is building a robot finger with a ball at the tip. The ball will roll over an object. It will tell the difference between smooth and rough surfaces.

Some of these fingers are hooked up to gloves worn by humans. These robots send information they feel to the gloves. Then the humans wearing the gloves can feel what the robots feel. This could help in exploring space.

Another team has made a robot that looks like a sea creature. It is called Public Anemone. This creature can already move and see. Now the scientists are making its "skin." The skin will be able to sense heat, pressure, and movement.

Robot research is not just for fun. Robots can do jobs that are too hard, dangerous, or dull for humans. To do these jobs, robots must move, see, and feel.

Name _____ Date_____

1. What will likely happen if a robot finger lifts a feather?
Ⓐ It will drop the feather.   Ⓑ It will use a gentle grip.
Ⓒ It will hold it tightly.   Ⓓ It will break the feather.

2. Based on the passage, which task is a job robots might do in the future?
Ⓐ train dogs   Ⓑ design houses
Ⓒ place explosives   Ⓓ paint portraits

3. If a future robot touched a rock on Mars, what might happen?
Ⓐ The rock would send electricity through the robot.
Ⓑ Plastic would cause the robot to explode.
Ⓒ It would break the rock with its fingertips.
Ⓓ A scientist on Earth wearing a glove would feel the rock's texture.

4. According to the passage, what will Public Anemone soon be able to do?

_____

_____

5. In the future, what kinds of "dull" jobs will robots do? Describe at least two such jobs.

_____

_____

Name _____ Date _____

Directions: Read the passage. Then use the information from the passage to answer questions 1–5.

Sally Ride, Scientist and Space Explorer

Have you ever wanted to spend a week in a small room with four other people? That's how it is in a space shuttle. Flying in a tiny spaceship isn't easy, and only the best are chosen for it. Sally Ride is one of them. She was the first U.S. woman in space.

Once, Sally wanted to be a tennis player. Then she got interested in science. She worked hard to become a scientist. In 1978, she was chosen from 8,000 people to be an astronaut. Astronauts spend years training before they go into space. They have to be able to handle anything that happens. From flying jets to fixing radios, she did it all. Astronauts also have special jobs. One of her jobs was running a robot arm she had helped to make.

In June 1983, Dr. Ride got to put all her training to work. She and four other astronauts took off and spent a week in the space shuttle *Challenger*. In her book *To Space and Back*, she described what it was like to float hundreds of miles above Earth. The next year she flew on the *Challenger* again. She was training for a third trip when the *Challenger* blew up. Everyone on board that day was killed.

Today, Sally Ride teaches science at the University of California. She also helps girls who want to become scientists. She knows what it is like to have big dreams. She also knows that other people can help you make them come true.

Name _____ Date _____

1. You can guess that as a girl, Sally Ride probably was _____.

Ⓐ not very interested in school

Ⓑ good at sports

Ⓒ the friendliest person in her class

Ⓓ afraid of flying

2. Which of these would Sally Ride most likely say to a girl who wants to be a scientist?

Ⓐ "You should try playing tennis."

Ⓑ "Not many girls get to be astronauts."

Ⓒ "You can do whatever you set your mind to."

Ⓓ "If you can't be a scientist, try tennis."

3. If you looked through Sally Ride's book, *To Space and Back*, you would most likely see pictures of _____.

Ⓐ how Earth looks from space

Ⓑ Sally Ride playing tennis

Ⓒ where the University of California is located

Ⓓ Sally Ride's parents

4. If Sally Ride had not become an astronaut, what would she probably have done?

_____

5. Sally Ride was the first U.S. woman in space. How did her experiences probably affect the chances of other women becoming astronauts?

_____

_____

Directions: Read the passage. Then use the information from the passage to answer questions 1–5.

A Look at Lakes

A lake is a body of water surrounded by land. When a hollow fills with water, a lake is made. Some lakes form in old volcanoes. One such lake is Crater Lake in Oregon. Many lakes form in holes left by glaciers. People also make lakes by building dams. Lake Mead is one lake made this way. It was formed when Hoover Dam was built on the Colorado River.

Lakes fill up with water from rivers and streams that run into them. Rain and melted snow also help fill up lakes. The water that runs into lakes often flows above ground. It is easy to see. But some lakes seem to fill up as if by magic. These lakes are fed by springs and streams that flow underground.

Most lakes have freshwater, but some are salty, like the ocean. Great Salt Lake in Utah is salty. Saltwater lakes are found in hot, dry places. Heat causes the water in these lakes to evaporate. Small amounts of salt in the water are left behind. Over many years, the salt builds up in the lake.

Lakes don't last forever. A lake may dry up if the climate gets hotter. When this happens, more water evaporates than flows in. Other lakes dry up because the rivers and streams that feed them change course. Some disappear because they slowly fill up with mud and plants.

Name _____ Date_____

1. Which sentence best summarizes what this passage is about?

Ⓐ   It describes one lake.

Ⓑ   It compares two lakes.

Ⓒ   It explains why lakes are important.

Ⓓ   It tells how lakes form and change.

2. Which detail should be included in a summary of the first paragraph?

Ⓐ   Lakes may form in holes left by volcanoes or glaciers.

Ⓑ   Lakes fed by underground streams are quite cold.

Ⓒ   Many lakes are kept filled by streams running into them.

Ⓓ   Hoover Dam was built across the Colorado River.

3. Read these two sentences from the passage.

But some lakes seem to fill up as if by magic. These lakes are fed by springs and streams that flow underground.

Which is the best paraphrase of these sentences?

Ⓐ   Some lakes are magical lakes underground.

Ⓑ   These lakes fill by magic from springs and streams.

Ⓒ   Some lakes are fed by underground springs or streams.

Ⓓ   Springs and streams sometimes form lakes underground.

4. Write one or two sentences that summarize the third paragraph.

_____

_____

5. Rewrite these sentences in your own words.

A lake may dry up if the climate gets hotter. When this happens, more water evaporates than flows in.

_____

_____

Directions: Read the passage. Then use the information from the passage to answer questions 1–5.

Measuring Time

People are very interested in time. They have been measuring time for thousands of years. The first "clocks" were sticks in the ground. The sticks cast shadows when the sun was out. The shadows helped people know what time it was. Then, around 1500 B.C. in Egypt, the sundial was invented. It also used the sun to tell time. It was more precise than the stick clock. People used sundials for 3,000 years.

The water clock was used around the same time. It was a stone pot with sloping sides. Water dripped out of a hole in the bottom. The amount that was left told people how much time had gone by. This clock did not rely on the sun, so it could be used at night.

Around A.D. 900, people began using candle clocks. A candle clock was a candle with marks on it. When the candle burned down to a mark, this showed that a certain amount of time had passed.

The sandglass was first used in the 1300s. It had a shape like the number 8. Sand was placed in the top part and ran through to the bottom. When all the sand had gone through, a certain amount of time had passed.

The first real clocks were very large and did not keep time very well. Later, clocks were made using springs. They were smaller and kept better time.

In the 1920s, quartz crystals were used in clocks. These clocks had no gears to wind or break. Most clocks today are made with quartz crystals.

Name _____ Date_____

1. Which idea should be included in a summary of this passage?

Ⓐ   Sundials used the sun to tell time.

Ⓑ   The sundial was invented long ago.

Ⓒ   Sand was placed in the top part.

Ⓓ   A candle clock was just a candle.

2. Which sentence best paraphrases the first two sentences in paragraph four?

Ⓐ   When all the sand has gone through, a certain amount of time has passed.

Ⓑ   Quartz crystals are very precise.

Ⓒ   In the 1300s, people began to use the sandglass.

Ⓓ   Clocks today have no gears to wind or break.

3. Which idea does NOT belong in a summary of this passage?

Ⓐ   A candle burning down showed the passing of time.

Ⓑ   Early clocks were large and did not keep time well.

Ⓒ   In the sandglass, sand running through the glass marked an amount of time.

Ⓓ   The water clock had sloping sides.

4. Write a summary of the first four paragraphs.

_____

_____

5. Write a summary of the last two paragraphs.

_____

_____

Name _____ Date _____

Directions: Read the passage. Then use the information from the passage to answer questions 1–5.

Calendars

The Western calendar that we use today began in Rome more than 2,000 years ago.

The Western Calendar

Around 45 B.C., Julius Caesar was the ruler of Rome. He called for a new calendar. It was called the Julian calendar. It was based on the lunar cycle, or the time it takes the moon to orbit Earth. It is also the time it takes the moon to go from a new moon to a full moon and back to a new moon again. That is about 29½ days. A year in the Julian calendar measures the days by one orbit of Earth around the sun. That is about 365 days.

The Julian calendar was fairly accurate. But it lost one day every 128 years. By 1582, it was ten days off. Pope Gregory XIII corrected it by adding an extra day to the month of February every four years. This is what we call a "leap year." This new system was called the Gregorian calendar.

Other Calendars

Different calendars are used by people around the world. They include the Chinese, Islamic, and Hebrew calendars. All three are based on lunar cycles.

The Chinese calendar has 12 or 13 months each year. The calendar goes for 60 years. Then it begins again.

The Islamic, or Muslim, calendar goes for three years and then begins again. It has 12 months. Each month has either 29 or 30 days.

The Hebrew calendar has 12 months each year. Each month has 29 or 30 days. In leap years, an extra month of 29 days is added.

Name _____ Date _____

1. The first two paragraphs of this passage tell mostly about _____.
- (A) how Earth travels around the sun
- (B) why Julius Caesar was the ruler of Rome
- (C) how the Julian calendar came to be
- (D) what the moon looks like

2. Write one or two sentences summarizing the information in the first part of the passage, "The Western Calendar."

_____

_____

3. The second half of the passage tells mostly about _____.
- (A) Pope Gregory XIII
- (B) holidays in the Chinese calendar
- (C) Hebrew numbers
- (D) examples of other calendars

4. Which is the best description of how the Islamic calendar works?
- (A) It is a lunar calendar with 12 months in a year and 29 or 30 days in each month.
- (B) It is sometimes called the Muslim calendar, and it is based on lunar cycles.
- (C) It is similar to the Chinese and Hebrew calendars in that they are all lunar calendars.
- (D) It is a three-year calendar with 29 or 30 days in each month.

5. Read the sentence from the passage. Write a paraphrase of this sentence in your own words.

"It is also the time it takes the moon to go from a new moon to a full moon and back to a new moon again."

_____

Name_____ Date _____

Directions: Read the passage. Then use the information from the passage to answer questions 1–5.

Circus Smirkus

Have you ever wanted to join the circus? Well, you can—at least for the summer.

Circus Smirkus is a circus for young people ages 10 to 20. You can try out for the circus. You can learn to juggle, walk on a wire, tumble, or be a clown. If you are good enough, you can spend the summer traveling with the circus.

Circus Smirkus was founded in the small town of Greensboro, Vermont. Young people from all over the world join the circus each year. Some even go to the Circus Camp in Craftsbury Common, Vermont. For one or two weeks, they learn circus skills. The best performers join the traveling circus group for the Summer Big Top Tour. Kids in this group train in June, after school has ended. Then they travel around New England and New York in July and August.

The Big Top Tour goes to 15 places each year. It gives 72 shows. Kids in the group help with all the work. They even set up the tent and sell tickets. Most of the money from ticket sales goes to support local programs, such as day-care centers and museums.

Joining Circus Smirkus is a great way to learn circus skills—and have a lot of fun!

Important Dates in Circus Smirkus History

1987: Circus Smirkus is founded by Rob Mermin, a circus clown.

1988: Circus Smirkus holds first Summer Big Top Tour.

1993: Summer Big Top Tour includes guests from Russia and ten Native American groups.

1997: Summer Tour plays 60 shows in New England.

2000: Circus Smirkus TV series is shown on Disney Channel.

2005: Smirkus School of Circus Arts opens in Essex, VT.

Name _____ Date_____

1. In what year was Circus Smirkus started?

Ⓐ 1987

Ⓑ 1988

Ⓒ 1999

Ⓓ 2001

2. What did Circus Smirkus do for the first time in 1988?

Ⓐ It was founded by Rob Mermin.

Ⓑ It included Native American performers.

Ⓒ It held a Summer Big Top Tour.

Ⓓ It opened a school of circus arts.

3. In what year did Circus Smirkus appear in a TV series?

Ⓐ 1987

Ⓑ 1993

Ⓒ 1997

Ⓓ 2000

4. What happened to Circus Smirkus in 2005?

_____

_____

5. Write two or three sentences describing the Summer Big Top Tour.

_____

_____

Name _____ Date _____

Directions: Read the passage. Then use the information from the passage to answer questions 1–5.

Homemade Homes

In the United States, most of the materials used to build homes are made in factories and mills. However, there are other kinds of homes. All around the world, people build homes from natural materials. Here are some examples.

Adobe house

This is a brick house. The bricks are made of adobe, which is a mixture of soil, clay, straw, and water. The bricks are dried in the sun. The roof of the house is made from wooden poles covered with brush and more adobe. Adobe houses are widely used in Mexico, the southwestern United States, and northern Africa.

Bedouin tent

This tent is made from woven goat hair. The roof is stretched over rows of wooden poles. The tent may be left open, or side cloths may be hung from the roof. Bedouin tents are used mainly in the deserts of Africa and Asia.

Yurt

This round house has a dome-shaped roof and walls made from pieces of wood tied together. Roof poles are placed on top of these walls. The house is covered with thick felt made from sheep's wool. Yurts are used in the wide open plains of Russia and Mongolia.

Name _____ Date_____

1. You can tell from the descriptions that all three kinds of homes are built with _____.

Ⓐ clay   Ⓑ wood

Ⓒ wool   Ⓓ grass

2. Which kind of home has a flat roof?

Ⓐ tropical house   Ⓑ Bedouin tent

Ⓒ adobe house   Ⓓ yurt

3. Which kind of home does not have walls?

Ⓐ tropical house   Ⓑ Bedouin tent

Ⓒ adobe house   Ⓓ yurt

4. Name one or two ways in which the yurt and the Bedouin tent look similar.

_____

_____

5. How are most homes in the United States different from the homes shown in the pictures?

_____

_____

Name _____ Date _____

Directions: Read the passage. Then use the information from the passage to answer questions 1–5.

The Underground Railroad

Before the Civil War, slavery was legal in some states but not in others. George Washington had slaves in Virginia. In 1786, a group of people called Quakers helped one of his slaves escape. These Quakers were part of a secret system that moved slaves to the North and to Canada. Slavery was illegal in Canada, so the slaves would be free. Later, this system became known as the Underground Railroad. Helping slaves escape was illegal. So it had to be secret, or "underground."

Like a real railroad, this one had stations. These were hiding places where people could rest and eat. Conductors moved the runaways between stations. Harriet Tubman was a conductor. She had escaped from the South. Then she went back. She risked her life many times to bring more slaves to freedom.

Runaways often traveled by night, mostly on foot. They followed the North Star. Often they traveled in winter. Then they could walk across frozen rivers. It could take a year to reach Canada. Some took a path through Ohio. Others went through Maryland or Pennsylvania. Many people took great risks to help slaves escape.

The end of the Civil War brought an end to slavery. But before that, up to 100,000 slaves rode to freedom on the Underground Railroad.

Slavery in America

1776	1784	1793	1820	1830	1849	1861–1865
Declaration of Independence	Congress keeps slavery legal.	Congress makes it illegal to help slaves escape.	Slavery was made illegal in new northern states.	Underground Railroad begins.	Harriet Tubman escapes.	Civil War

Name _____ Date _____

1. Which event happened first?

Ⓐ The Civil War started.

Ⓑ The Underground Railroad began.

Ⓒ Congress voted to keep slavery legal.

Ⓓ Harriet Tubman escaped.

2. What did Congress decide in 1793?

_____

_____

3. What happened in 1849?

Ⓐ The Declaration of Independence was written.

Ⓑ The Civil War began.

Ⓒ Slavery became illegal.

Ⓓ Harriet Tubman escaped from the South.

4. What change took place in 1820?

_____

_____

5. When did slavery come to an end in the United States?

Ⓐ 1830

Ⓑ 1849

Ⓒ 1865

Ⓓ 1870

Name_____ Date _____

Directions: Read the passage. Then use the information from the passage
to answer questions 1–5.

Traveling Plants

Like many things in nature, "traveling" plants seem almost magical. But once you learn how these plants reproduce and grow, the magic will make sense.

Flowering plants produce seeds. Seeds are baby plants. These seeds are carried here and there in different ways.

Wind Some plant seeds are light and feathery. They can be carried a long way by the wind. The seeds of dandelions, milkweed, and maple trees are examples.

Dandelion and maple seeds travel on the wind.

Animals and People Other plant seeds stick to animal fur or people's clothes. Then they are carried to new places. These plants include plantain, burdock, and Queen Anne's lace.

Water Some plants drop their seeds into water. Then the seeds float away. The water lily and the coconut tree spread their seeds in this way. Unlike most seeds, the seeds from a coconut tree can live in salt water.

The leaves of water lilies are covered with jelly cases, which hold seeds. When the cases float away, the jelly melts, releasing the seeds.

Although seeds travel in different ways, the results are the same. When the seeds reach their new homes, some of them take root. These seeds grow into new plants. Then the new plants make more seeds.

Name _____ Date_____

1. Which kind of plant seed travels by wind?

(A) coconut tree   (B) Queen Anne's lace

(C) maple tree   (D) plantain

2. How do the seeds of water lilies travel?

(A) They float by water.   (B) They stick to animals.

(C) They float through the air. (D) They stick to people's clothes.

3. How are all the seeds in the passage alike?

(A) They all stick to animals.   (B) They all grow in ponds.

(C) They all travel.   (D) They all float in the air.

4. How do jelly cases help seeds travel?

_____

_____

5. List three kinds of seeds that are carried by animals and people.

_____

_____

Directions: Read the passage. Then use the information from the passage to answer questions 1–5.

Use Your Beach Treasures

Do you like to find things on the beach? Do you pick up pretty shells and stones? Here are some ways to use and enjoy your beach treasures.

Sand *Make an outdoor sand lantern.** Open up a large paper bag. Fold the top down about six inches. Put five or six inches of sand in the bag. Place a candle in the sand. When it is dark, have a grown-up light the candle. Enjoy!

Pebbles *Make a pebble picture.* Collect a lot of interesting beach pebbles. Draw a picture on cardboard. Arrange pretty colored pebbles on the picture. Glue on the pebbles and let the glue dry overnight. Make a hole and hang your pebble picture with string. Enjoy!

Shells *Make some shell chimes.* Gather a lot of small shells with holes. Cut pieces of string about 12 inches long. Put one or more shells on each string. Tie knots to hold the shells in place. Now fasten all the strings to a stick or piece of wood. Hang your chimes by a window. Open the window so the wind rings the chimes. Enjoy!

Beach Glass *Make a beach glass ornament.* Find smooth, colored pieces of glass. Get a piece of clear plastic, such as a coffee can lid. Glue on the glass pieces. When the glue is dry, make a hole near one side. Hang your ornament with string. Hang it by a window so light comes through. Enjoy!

*A *lantern* is a kind of light or lamp.

Name _____ Date_____

1. What does the writer say to make from shells?

Ⓐ a picture   Ⓑ an ornament

Ⓒ chimes   Ⓓ a lantern

2. What part of the selection tells how to make a picture?

Ⓐ **Sand**   Ⓑ **Pebbles**

Ⓒ **Shells**   Ⓓ **Beach Glass**

3. Why should you hang a beach glass ornament near a window?

Ⓐ to be safe

Ⓑ so the wind can blow it

Ⓒ to help the glue dry

Ⓓ so light comes through

4. What is a *lantern*?

_____

_____

5. Name three kinds of beach treasures from this passage. Tell what you can do with each kind of treasure.

_____

_____

_____

_____

Name _____ Date _____

Directions: Read the passage. Then use the information from the passage to answer questions 1–5.

Exploring the Deep

At 29,030 feet, Mount Everest is the highest point on Earth. It is in Asia. The highest point in North America is Mount McKinley in Alaska (20,320 feet). Do you know where the lowest point is? If you think about it, you'll realize it has to be in the ocean.

Challenger Deep

The lowest point on Earth is called Challenger Deep. It is 36,000 feet below sea level in the Mariana Trench. This is a valley in the Pacific Ocean near the Philippines. In 1960, two men went nearly to the bottom of Challenger Deep in a U.S. Navy submersible. (A submersible is a small underwater craft used for deep ocean exploring.) No one has gone back there since.

Exploring the Ocean Floor

Scientists can explore most of the ocean floor in submersibles. But going much deeper than 20,000 feet is very difficult for people. That's what ROVs are used for: to go where people can't. (ROVs are robots used to explore the ocean. They are run remotely from a ship. They take pictures and pick things up.) ROVs like sea-tractors can do things that people can't. (A sea-tractor is an ROV that rolls along the ocean floor.) Some can stay under water for six months.

Galápagos Rift

Another deep place is the Galápagos Rift near Ecuador, in the Pacific Ocean. The rift is 7,500 feet below sea level. In 1977, scientists found something new there—hot springs. They rise from the ocean floor. The water is hot because of nearby volcanoes. All around the springs live strange giant worms. We are still learning how these worms can live without sunlight.

Progress-Monitoring Comprehension Strategy Assessments ❹   ©2009 Newmark Learning, LLC

Name _____ Date _____

1. How far below sea level is the bottom of Challenger Deep?
Ⓐ 7,500 feet
Ⓑ 20,000 feet
Ⓒ 29,000 feet
Ⓓ 36,000 feet

2. What is a sea-tractor used for?
Ⓐ exploring the ocean floor
Ⓑ taking pictures of fish
Ⓒ looking for sunlight
Ⓓ working on fish farms

3. What is a submersible?
Ⓐ a strange giant worm
Ⓑ an underwater hot spring
Ⓒ an underwater craft used in deep water
Ⓓ a low point in the ocean

4. What is the Galápagos Rift, and where is it located?

_____

_____

5. What are ROVs, and what can they do?

_____

_____

Answer Key

Analyze Character
Grade 3
First on the Courts
1. D
2. A
3. C
4. Examples: After quitting school, she later went back to get her diploma. Or, she kept practicing hard to become a better tennis player.
5. Possible answers: Yes, Althea Gibson was a sports legend. She worked hard and was very determined. She overcame hardship to become a winner. Her courage helped those who came after her.

The Contest
1. B
2. C
3. D
4. Example: She will not mind because she is more interested in the quarters and the states than in winning the contest.
5. Possible responses: She is a neat and careful worker. She looks at everything carefully and likes to learn about things. She has good ideas, such as looking for coins in the car.

Grade 4
Elizabeth Cady Stanton
1. B
2. D
3. C
4. Example: None of the women delegates at the World's Anti-Slavery Convention got a seat.
5. Examples: She led the women's rights convention. She wrote and presented statements for a Declaration of Rights.

Analyze Story Elements
Grade 3
Buried Alive
1. D
2. C
3. B
4. The dog identified where the skier was buried.
5. Example: Rescuers dug him out of the snow and strapped him into a sled. Then they took him down the mountain.

A Long Week
1. A
2. C
3. B
4. Examples: Mama does not smile. She does not eat. She is very hot. She does not hear anything. She has been asleep for six days.
5. Possible response: Rebecca will ride her pony to town and bring back the doctor. Papa will stay home and take care of Mama.

Grade 4
The Wall
1. C
2. A
3. D
4. Example: Persa smiled at Gwen and told her she did a good job.
5. Example: She felt clumsy at the beginning but more confident at the end.

Analyze Text Structure and Organization
Grade 3
The Channel Tunnel
1. A
2. C
3. B
4. Examples: They worked together and shared the costs. They started digging from each end and met in the middle.
5. People could now take their cars from England to France and back.

Comics Then and Now
1. C
2. D
3. A
4. Example: You can find out from the fourth paragraph, which tells of the first comic book about a superhero.
5. Example: The title shows that the subject is comics. The words then and now suggest that the passage tells how comics have changed.

Grade 4
Land of Ice and Snow
1. D
2. B
3. C
4. Example: You can see more kinds of whales and seals there. You can see emperor and Adélie penguins.
5. Example: No countries own Antarctica. They have agreed to share it and keep it as it is.

Answer Key

Compare and Contrast
Grade 3
Leonardo da Vinci: Master of Invention
1. B
2. D
3. B
4. It was used to move air.
5. Example: An airplane and the flying ship both fly through the air, have wings, and carry people.

A Different Kind of Ride
1. A
2. C
3. D
4. Example: Most people ride near home in warm weather, but Doug rides on ice and snow in Antarctica.
5. Example: Doug's bike has very fat tires, it has no plastic parts, it costs more money, and it only works well on ice and snow.

Grade 4
Kangaroos and Opossums
1. C
2. C
3. D
4. Example: Both eat plants. Kangaroos eat mostly grass, but opossums eat leaves, fruit, bugs, and other things.
5. Example: Kangaroos spend their time on the ground; opossums spend some time in trees.

Evaluate Fact and Opinion
Grade 3
The Most Exciting Job in the World
1. B
2. B
3. C
4. Examples of facts: The probe worked for hours. Scientists are studying information from the probe.
It will take many years to study the information. Examples of opinions: The probe would work for only a few minutes. It was very exciting.
5. Example: A good scientist must like to learn new things, be curious, and be patient.

New Video Fun from Giant Games
1. D
2. B
3. D
4. Example: "Build-A-World and Build-A-Team cost $30.00 each." This is a fact because it can be verified.
5. Example: "Build-A-Team is a ton of fun!" This is an opinion because it expresses a personal feeling and cannot be verified from the text.

Grade 4
The Sox and the Bambino
1. D
2. C
3. A
4. It expresses an opinion: "a wonderful thing happened."
5. The student writes a sentence and tells whether it is a fact or an opinion.

Draw Conclusions
Grade 3
Growing Up Shawnee
1. B
2. D
3. C
4. Example: They had to learn different things. The boys spent their time hunting, while the girls prepared food and made clothing.
5. Example: "They learned to tan animal hides and make pots out of clay".

Trains of the Future
1. A
2. C
3. C
4. Examples: Maglev trains are expensive. Some people think they are not very practical.
5. Example: Power from the electromagnets lifts the train so it does not actually run on the track.

Grade 4
Pests
1. D
2. B
3. C
4. Example: Zebra mussels came from outside the United States.
5. Examples: Plant seeds can travel on shoes. Animals can come in as pets. Insects can travel on airplanes, cars, or ships.

Answer Key

Evaluate Author's Purpose and Point of View
Grade 3

A Sweet Time of Year
1. A
2. B
3. D
4. Example: The author thinks it is a great time of year. He says, "Making syrup is fun" and "Syrup makers love this time of year."
5. Example: The author loves maple syrup. "It smells wonderful, and it tastes great."

From the Police Chief's Mailbag
1. C
2. A
3. B
4. Example: She wants the chief to call and say he will help.
5. Examples: She thinks children should be able to ride. She thinks it is fun. She thinks it is not safe without a crossing guard.

Grade 4

Living on a Kibbutz
1. D
2. B
3. C
4. Example: The author seems to think it's a great idea. He says that everyone acted like one big family.
5. Examples: "It was a wonderful way of life!" "Life on a kibbutz today is sadly much different from in the past."

Identify Cause and Effect
Grade 3

The Tundra
1. B
2. A
3. D
4. Reasons: People are driving snowmobiles and cars into the area, and people are hunting the animals.
5. Example: Plants die, animals lack food, and the number of animals gets smaller.

Helping Some Big Babies
1. B
2. C
3. B
4. Reasons: Farmers kill elephants that get on their farms. Hunters kill elephants to get ivory.
5. Possible answers: No one would buy ivory. Hunters could not sell ivory. No one would hunt elephants. There would be fewer orphan elephants.

Grade 4

Sailing to California
1. C
2. B
3. D
4. Example: The wind got stronger and the wagon gained speed going downhill.
5. Example: They got angry with Zeb Thomas and ran him out of town.

Identify Main Idea and Supporting Details
Grade 3

The Great Pyramid
1. A
2. C
3. B
4. Early visitors stole nearly everything from the Great Pyramid.
5. Possible answers: King Khufu lived around 2,500 B.C. He had the Great Pyramid built. He ruled for about 20 years. He may have been a bad ruler who forced his people to build the pyramid.

Become a Cloud Watcher
1. A
2. C
3. D
4. Examples: They bring bad weather. They bring rain or hail. They may bring thunder and lightning. They may bring tornadoes.
5. Answers will vary. Examples: "Clouds and Weather," "Watching the Clouds."

Grade 4

The Lost Colony
1. C
2. D
3. Example: A second group of colonists settled in Roanoke in 1587.
4. B
5. Examples: When he returned, the people were gone. None of the colonists were ever seen again.

Answer Key

Identify Sequence or Steps in a Process
Grade 3

Making a Budget
1. C
2. D
3. B
4. Example: Write all necessary expenses, or money you must spend.
5. Example: Figure out how much money came in and how much you spent. Then fill in the boxes on the chart under "What Really Happened."

All Mixed Up
1. C
2. D
3. A
4. Example: The water particles move around, and the food-coloring particles blend together.
5. Possible answer: Dispose of the orange water, clean the jar, and clean up the area where you did the experiment.

Grade 4

A Long Journey
1. D
2. B
3. A
4. Example: The monarchs begin to move north again.
5. Examples: First, they lay eggs along the way. Then (or finally) they reach their summer homes.

Make Inferences
Grade 3

Just Not Herself
1. B
2. D
3. A
4. Hank's phone number and a picture of Snowshoes
5. Hank named her Snowshoes because she had white paws.

Harriet the Tortoise
1. A
2. D
3. B
4. Possible answers: Harriet lived in comfort. She was fed a healthful diet of plants.
5. Examples: She was old and might have suffered from being ridden; The zookeepers wanted to take care of her and keep her safe.

Grade 4

Mapping the Pacific
1. A
2. D
3. B
4. Example: It was hard to keep food fresh on long trips. They didn't have refrigerators and couldn't get fresh food if they didn't stop anywhere.
5. Example: Almost no one had been to the Pacific Ocean. People thought there might be a continent in the South Pacific and land at the South Pole, but they did not know.

Make Predictions
Grade 3

She Says, He Says
1. C
2. A
3. D
4. He will bring his sand toys.
5. Example: Each of them will find out that the other can't swim well.

Giving Robots a Sense of Touch
1. B
2. C
3. D
4. Example: It will be able to sense or feel heat, pressure, and movement through its skin.
5. Possible answer: Robots will do repetitive, boring jobs that people have trouble doing, such as assembly line work in a factory or packing boxes in a plant.

Grade 4

Sally Ride, Scientist and Space Explorer
1. B
2. C
3. A
4. Examples: She would have become a scientist, a science teacher, or perhaps a writer.
5. Example: Her experience probably increased other women's chances because she paved the way and served as a role model.

Answer Key

Summarize or Paraphrase Information
Grade 3
A Look at Lakes
1. D
2. A
3. C
4. Example: Saltwater lakes are found in hot, dry climates. Evaporation of water causes salt to build up in these lakes.
5. Example: A lake may dry up from a hot climate. The water in the lake evaporates faster than water flows in.

Measuring Time
1. A
2. C
3. D
4. Possible answer: The first ways to measure time were sticks and sundials that used the sun. These were used for 3,000 years. Then, starting around A.D. 900, candle clocks measured time as they burned down. Sandglasses measured time as sand passed through them.
5. Example: Early clocks were big and inaccurate. Springs allowed them to be smaller and more precise. Since the 1920s, most clocks have been made with quartz crystals.

Grade 4
Calendars
1. C
2. Example: The calendar we use is based on the Julian calendar of ancient Rome.
3. D
4. A
5. Example: It is the time of a full cycle of the moon from new to full and back again.

Use Graphic Features to Interpret Information
Grade 3
Circus Smirkus
1. A
2. C
3. D
4. The Smirkus School of Circus Arts opened in Essex, VT.
5. Example: The Big Top Tour is a traveling circus group. It goes to 15 towns and gives 72 shows during the summer.

Homemade Homes
1. B
2. C
3. B
4. Examples: They are both round; both are more or less dome-shaped; both have flexible or removable walls.
5. Examples: Most homes in the United States are rectangular with peaked or sloped roofs; most are built with factory materials; most are permanent, not moveable.

Grade 4
The Underground Railroad
1. C
2. It was illegal to help slaves escape.
3. D
4. Slavery became illegal in new northern states.
5. C

Use Text Features to Locate Information
Grade 3
Traveling Plants
1. C
2. A
3. C
4. Example: When the jelly case floats away, the jelly melts and the seeds are released.
5. Plantain, burdock, and Queen Anne's lace

Use Your Beach Treasures
1. C
2. B
3. D
4. a kind of light or lamp
5. Examples: With sand you can make a lantern; you can make a picture with pebbles; you can make chimes with shells or an ornament with beach glass.

Grade 4
Exploring the Deep
1. D
2. A
3. C
4. It is a deep place in the Pacific Ocean near Ecuador.
5. Example: ROVs are robots used to take pictures under water and pick things up from the ocean floor.

Scoring Chart

Student Name _____ Grade _____

Strategy	Test 1 Date / Score	Test 2 Date / Score	Test 3 Date / Score	Notes
Analyze Character	Date: _____ / 5	Date: _____ / 5	Date: _____ / 5	
Analyze Story Elements	Date: _____ / 5	Date: _____ / 5	Date: _____ / 5	
Analyze Text Structure and Organization	Date: _____ / 5	Date: _____ / 5	Date: _____ / 5	
Compare and Contrast	Date: _____ / 5	Date: _____ / 5	Date: _____ / 5	
Evaluate Fact and Opinion	Date: _____ / 5	Date: _____ / 5	Date: _____ / 5	
Draw Conclusions	Date: _____ / 5	Date: _____ / 5	Date: _____ / 5	
Evaluate Author's Purpose and Point of View	Date: _____ / 5	Date: _____ / 5	Date: _____ / 5	
Identify Cause and Effect	Date: _____ / 5	Date: _____ / 5	Date: _____ / 5	
Identify Main Idea and Supporting Details	Date: _____ / 5	Date: _____ / 5	Date: _____ / 5	
Identify Sequence or Steps in a Process	Date: _____ / 5	Date: _____ / 5	Date: _____ / 5	
Make Inferences	Date: _____ / 5	Date: _____ / 5	Date: _____ / 5	
Make Predictions	Date: _____ / 5	Date: _____ / 5	Date: _____ / 5	
Summarize Information	Date: _____ / 5	Date: _____ / 5	Date: _____ / 5	
Use Graphic Features to Interpret Information	Date: _____ / 5	Date: _____ / 5	Date: _____ / 5	
Use Text Features to Locate Information	Date: _____ / 5	Date: _____ / 5	Date: _____ / 5	